THE CHILDREN'S WORKER'S ENCYCLOPEDIA OF BIBLE-TEACHING IDEAS:

New Testament

Loveland, Colorado

The Children's Worker's Encyclopedia of Bible-Teaching Ideas:
New Testament
Copyright © 1997 Group Publishing, Inc.

Credits
Book Acquisitions Editor: Mike Nappa
Editors: Susan L. Lingo, Jody Brolsma, and Jan Kershner
Senior Editor: Lois Keffer
Chief Creative Officer: Joani Schultz
Copy Editor: Debbie Gowensmith
Art Directors: Lisa Chandler and Kari K. Monson
Cover Art Director: Helen H. Lannis
Computer Graphic Artist: Rosalie Lawrence
Cover Designer: Jean Bruns
Illustrators: Amy Bryant and Dana Regan
Production Manager: Ann Marie Gordon

Unless otherwise noted, Scriptures quoted from The Youth Bible, New Century Version, copyright © 1991 by Word Publishing, Dallas, Texas 75039. Used by permission.

Library of Congress Cataloging-in-Publication Data

The children's worker's encyclopedia of Bible-teaching ideas. New
    Testament.
        p.   cm.
    Includes indexes.
    ISBN 1-55945-625-6
    1. Bible. N.T.–Study and teaching–Handbooks, manuals, etc.
    2. Christian education of children–Handbooks, manuals, etc.
    3. Church work with children–Handbooks, manuals, etc.
    BS2530.C48 1997
    268'.432–dc20   96-34260
                                                                  CIP
                                                                   AC

10 9 8 7 6 5 4 3 2   06 05 04 03 02 01 00 99 98 97

Printed in the United States of America.

TABLE OF CONTENTS

CONTRIBUTORS

Many thanks to the following people, who loaned us their creative expertise to help bring together this volume of ideas:

Michelle Anthony
Jody Brolsma
Joyce Whitehead-Elliott
Lisa Flinn
Ellen Javernick
Christina Medina
Janet Miller
Jerayne Gray-Reneberg
Beth Wolf

INTRODUCTION

Once upon a time, the editors at a publishing house in Colorado had a dream. "What if," they said, "instead of simply *teaching* kids about the New Testament, we had a way to help them *experience* and apply the truths found in Scripture?"

So they went right to work. They contacted some of the most creative people in children's ministry and challenged them to develop exciting, inviting, New Testament–based activities and learning experiences for children. Then they compiled those ideas into this volume, *The Children's Worker's Encyclopedia of Bible-Teaching Ideas: New Testament.*

Suddenly, the book isn't just a dream. It's reality! And it's ready to be shared with children's workers around the world—children's workers like you.

In the following pages, you'll find bunches of active, guided experiences that take scriptural truths from the New Testament and bring them to life in your kids. Your children will gain a deeper understanding of the Bible through a variety of sensory and experiential activities including:

 learning games,

 object lessons,

 skits,

 prayers and quiet reflections,

 service projects and missions,

 affirmation activities,

 devotions,

 music ideas,

 parties,

 creative storytelling,

 trips 'n' travels,

and crafts and makables.

With such a wide variety of carefully planned, Scripture-focused activities, your children will look forward to spending time with the Bible. Not only will exciting activities spark their interests, but the truths they learn will change their lives.

The Children's Worker's Encyclopedia of Bible-Teaching Ideas: New Testament is an essential tool for any children's worker interested in helping children explore and understand the Bible. You can use the book with your group for Sunday school, children's church, midweek meetings, or any other time children are gathered together. So get ready for unique, motivating activities that will inspire your children to learn about the Bible and love the Bible in no time!

MATTHEW

" 'She will have a son, and they will name him Immanuel,' which means 'God is with us.' "

Matthew 1:23

MATTHEW 1:21-23

THEME:
We can serve God in many ways.

SUMMARY:
In this active DEVOTION, children will create "new" names for themselves which reflect ways to serve God.

PREPARATION: You'll need a Bible, index cards, markers, and tape.

EXPERIENCE
Have children form trios, and hand everyone an index card and a marker.

Say: **All of us have names that we're known by. Most of our names have certain meanings. Do any of you know what your name means?** Allow children who know the meanings of their names to share them with the class. You may wish to bring in a book of names so all the children can find the meanings of their names.

Say: **Did you know that Jesus has other names besides "Jesus"? Just as you or your friends may have nicknames, Jesus has different names, too. I'm going to read from the book of Matthew in the Bible. Listen for one of Jesus' other names. When you hear it, put your hand over your heart.** Read aloud Matthew 1:21-23.

Say: **Jesus has many names, and one of them is Immanuel.**

The name Immanuel means "God is with us." It tells us who Jesus is and that Jesus was born to live among us. Jesus also has names that tell who he is and how he serves God. Some of his names are "bread of life" (John 6:35), "good shepherd" (John 10:11), and the "way" and "truth" (John 14:6).

Think of ways you can serve God, such as helping, praying, and learning. Then create a "new" name for yourself that describes a way you can serve God. On your index card, write your new name and the way you can serve God. For example, if I want to serve God by singing, then my new name could be Songster or Tuneful.

Allow children several minutes to create their new names.

RESPONSE

Call time, then have each trio read aloud its cards. After all the children have read their cards, try to recall as many new names as possible. End by taping the cards to the children's clothes as name tags.

CLOSING

Ask all the children to stand and bow their heads.

Form a circle for the closing prayer. Say: **God of our service, we want to serve you the best way we can. Thank you for our abilities. Help us use them in good ways. Guide and strengthen** (name each child). **Amen.**

MATTHEW
2:1-12

THEME:
We can trust God to lead us in the right direction.

SUMMARY:
Kids take a mystery TRIP to learn about trusting God.

PREPARATION: You'll need a Bible.

Select a destination within walking distance, such as a local park, a children's amusement center, or somewhere within the church grounds. If weather doesn't permit outside activity, take a walk inside the church instead.

Say: **Today we're taking a mystery trip. I won't tell you where we're going, but I will tell you how we'll get there—with a big dose of trust! I will be the Guide, and you all will be the Travelers. Travelers, you'll close your eyes while I lead you along a path. You must hold the hand of the Traveler in front of you, and I'll hold the hand of the Traveler behind me. We'll make a long chain! Be careful to walk exactly where the person in front of you walks; we want to arrive at our destination safely.**

Taking your Bible, lead the children to the predetermined destination. Then ask:

■ **What was it like not knowing exactly where you were going?**

■ **Did you trust me as your Guide? Explain.**

■ **What might have happened**

if you hadn't followed the Traveler in front of you?

Hold up the Bible, and say: **Let's listen to a story about three people who went on a journey. They did not know where they were going, so they trusted a very special guide. Listen and see if you can figure out the identity of the special guide.** Read aloud Matthew 2:1-12, then ask:

■ **What was the reason for the wise men's trip?**

■ **Who was their special guide?**

■ **Were the wise men wise to trust God? Why?**

■ **How can we trust God in our travels through life?**

Say: **Many times in life, we feel mixed up and unsure about where we're going. It's important to know that we can trust God to lead us in the right direction.**

MATTHEW
2:1-12

THEME:
It's important to worship Jesus.

SUMMARY:
Use this SKIT to help children understand the importance of Jesus' birth and realize that he is worthy of our praise.

THE BABY SHOWER

SCENE: Three wise men are traveling across the desert.

PROPS: You'll need colorful scarves wrapped into three bundles, two jars of colored oil, a baby bottle, a rattle, a pacifier, a cloth or disposable diaper, baby powder, and a small container of water.

CHARACTERS:
Makir (a wise man dressed in robes, a turban, and jewelry)
Kanah (a wise man dressed in robes, a turban, and jewelry)
Asriel (a wise man dressed in robes, a turban, and jewelry)

SCRIPT
(Three wise men enter in single file. Makir, the first in line, drops his bundle and plops to the floor.)

Makir: That's it! I can't go any farther! I've got sand in my ears, dust in my eyes, and camel spit on my robe! Yuck!

Kanah: *(Pulling Makir's arm)* Makir, we've still got a long trip ahead of us—you can't stop here. *(Drops the arm.)* Fine, I'll water the camels while you rest. Then we must move on to Jerusalem. There's a—

Makir: *(Interrupting)* —a baby waiting there. Yeah, I know! But I'm so tired! Sometimes I wish we hadn't seen that big ol' star from the east.

Kanah: *(Sighs.)* I give up! Asriel, you try to make this wise guy understand. I'm going to water the camels. *(Walks offstage.)*

Makir: *(Shouting to Kanah)* Watch out for that fur-ball camel named Thirsty!
(From offstage, someone tosses a bit of water to splash onto the stage.)

Makir: *(Still shouting to Kanah)* He spits!

Kanah: *(Grumbling from offstage)* Thanks for the warning, Makir.

Asriel: Why so grumpy, Makir? You seemed excited when we set out. And I notice that you've brought a pretty big bundle of presents for the newborn king.

Makir: Well, I know babies need lots of diapers and stuff—especially when they're first born! I mean, my mom said I went through diapers like you wouldn't—

Asriel: *(Interrupting)* Diapers! You brought the newborn king diapers?

Makir: Sure! I mean, I know it's not a fancy gift, but—wait a minute! Did you and Kanah go in together to get him a stroller or something? That's just great. You'll make my gifts look cheap and unimportant.

Asriel: We...uh...didn't get him a stroller. Makir, I don't think you understand. This baby is very special, and we—

Makir: Well, I'm glad I picked up a few extra items then. *(Picks up bundle and begins to unpack baby items.)* See? I've purchased diapers, a bottle, a rattle, a pacifier, baby powder—*(Squeezes the powder, and it sprays on Kanah, who's just come to rejoin the group.)* Oops! Sorry, Kanah.

Kanah: *(Coughing and wiping away the powder)* What is all this stuff? Did someone find a sale at Ali's Tent of Toys?

Makir: I picked out these gifts myself. Are you making fun of them? What did you guys bring?

Asriel: *(Shaking head with disbelief)* Kanah, get our bags from the camels. Let's show Makir what we've brought for the special baby.

(Kanah exits. Again, someone tosses a bit of water to splash onto the stage.)

Kanah: Thirsty! You fur-ball of a camel! *(Enters, damp, with two expensive-looking bundles.)*

Asriel: You see, Makir, we're not just going to see any ol' baby. This baby is special. This baby is a king! One who will rule over nations and bring peace to the entire world. A savior like that deserves more than just a rattle or diapers. He's royalty! *(Pulls a jar of oil from his bundle and hands it to Makir.)*

Makir: You got him a bottle of baby shampoo?

Asriel: *(Shakes his head.)* No, no! This is frankincense.

Makir: Frank and who?

Asriel: Frankincense! It's an expensive perfume fit for a king.

Makir: He's just a baby!

Kanah: But the star *(pointing offstage)*—the star says he's a special baby. The King of the Jews. *(Opens bundle and brings out a jar.)* That's why I brought him myrrh, another rich perfume. This is a gift for a king...not a baby.

Makir: *(Miserably)* Why didn't you guys tell me? Now I'm stuck with a bundle of baby stuff, and I'm headed to see the most important king the world will ever know! I want to worship him too.

Asriel: But Makir, you don't understand. Any gift you offer this special king is fine. You just need to give your gifts in love!

Makir: Well, I do have this chest of gold pieces. My uncle asked me to get him a T-shirt that says, "My nephew went to Jerusalem, and all I got was—" Hey! Wait a minute! I'll give the baby king my gold! *(Pauses, then gathers the baby items quickly.)* Hurry, you guys! We've got to go see the king! What are you sitting there for? Jerusalem's a long way off.

Asriel: *(Smiling)* I think he understands all about the special king now.

(As wise men exit, the audience hears a splash of water; then all three wise men shout, "Thirsty!")

Permission to photocopy this skit from *The Children's Worker's Encyclopedia of Bible-Teaching Ideas: NT* granted for local church use. Copyright © Group Publishing, Inc., P.O. Box 481, Loveland, CO 80539.

If you use this skit as a discussion starter, here are possible questions:
■ **What gift can you give Jesus?**
■ **How are praise and worship like a gift we offer?**
■ **Why is it important to offer Jesus the best we have?**

MATTHEW 2:13-14

THEME:
God protects us because he loves us.

SUMMARY:
This CREATIVE STORYTELLING activity invites kids to join the flight to Egypt.

PREPARATION: You'll need a stack of old newspaper and tape.

Before beginning the story, invite children to crumple the newspaper into oblong "baby" bundles and wrap them with tape. If you don't have newspaper, have children cradle one of their shoes as a baby or pretend to hold a baby. You may wish to darken the room a bit to add suspense to this nighttime story. Encourage children to join you in doing the italicized motions.

GOD SENDS A WARNING

It's late at night in the town of Bethlehem. Joseph and Mary and baby Jesus are sound asleep. *(Lie on the floor and softly snore.)* **As Joseph sleeps, he has an amazing dream. Oh, look! An angel of the Lord is in the dream. What is the angel saying? Shh** *(put your finger to your lips)*, **listen carefully. The angel says, "Get up, Joseph! Wake the child and his mother, and go to Egypt, where you'll be safe. King Herod is searching for the baby and wants to kill him."**

Joseph wakes up and jumps to his feet. *(Hop up.)* **He must wake Mary. He calls, "Mary! Mary, wake up!** *(Cup hands around mouth.)* **We must leave Bethlehem. I know it's the middle of the night, but baby Jesus is in great danger. The angel said, 'Go to Egypt.' Now let's hurry!"** *(Pick up the newspaper "baby.")*

(Trudge around the room, carrying the baby bundle.) **There they are on the road to Egypt. Oh, it's a dark night to travel and such a long, long way to Egypt. But God will show them the way. They can count on God to help them. Oh, it seems like they'll never**

get there. *(Wipe your forehead and continue trudging along.)*

(Point ahead.) **Look! There's Egypt! God has led Mary and Joseph to Egypt, and baby Jesus is safe and sound.**

Have children form a circle. Say: **Joseph trusted God when he took his family to Egypt. Joseph and Mary knew that God loved them and would keep them all safe. And we can trust God to love us and help us, too. Yippee! Let's clap and cheer to show how glad we are that God loves us and protects us.** Lead children in a lively cheer.

MATTHEW
3:1-6

THEME:
We can prepare a place inside our hearts for Jesus.

SUMMARY:
In this OBJECT LESSON, water helps kids think about ways to prepare their hearts and lives for Jesus.

PREPARATION: You'll need a Bible, a two-quart pitcher of water, presweetened soft drink mix, six-ounce cups, and a mixing spoon.

Set the pitcher of water on a table, and have kids gather around. Ask:

■ **When was a time you got ready for a special visitor or guest?**

■ **How did you feel as you prepared for this special person?**

■ **What are some ways we could use water to prepare for a special visitor?**

Say: **In our Bible story today, we'll learn how John the Baptist used water to help people prepare for Jesus. Let's read aloud from Matthew 3:1-6.** Have volunteers read aloud Matthew 3:1-6, then ask:

■ **What did John the Baptist use water for?**

■ **Who was John preparing the way for?**

■ **Why did John want people to be ready for Jesus?**

■ **How can we prepare our hearts to love Jesus?**

Say: **John the Baptist wanted people to know that Jesus was coming. And John knew that people needed to be ready to accept Jesus' love into their hearts. We want our hearts to welcome Jesus, too. Let's pray.** Pray: **Dear God, thank you for sending John the Baptist to help people get ready for Jesus. Help us prepare our hearts for Jesus, too. Amen.**

Say: **Now let's use this water to prepare a special treat!** Mix presweetened soft drink mix into the pitcher of water. Let kids take turns stirring; then serve the treat in paper cups. You may wish to give each child a small packet of soft drink mix to take home as a reminder to prepare for Jesus.

MATTHEW
3:13-17

THEME:
God wants us to obey him.

SUMMARY:
In this active DEVOTION, kids brainstorm about ways to obey God.

PREPARATION: For this activity, you'll need a Bible.

Arrange for the children to visit the pastor at the pulpit or lectern for this activity. If you choose not to use a pulpit or lectern, have kids decorate a sturdy box to stand on instead.

EXPERIENCE

Gather children in the worship area. Have the pastor or children's minister stand at the pulpit or lectern and say: **Most of the time, I stand in this special place to speak to the congregation. I read from the Bible and teach about God and his special rules for living. But I don't make up the rules—God does! God has special rules about how he wants us to act. Today we'll brainstorm about ways we can obey God.**

Have children form groups of three, and allow them five minutes to brainstorm about three ways to obey God—going to church, honoring their parents, praying, being kind to others, or reading the Bible, for example. Circulate among the children, and help those who are having trouble think of ways to obey God.

RESPONSE

At the end of five minutes, call time. Invite each group to come to the pulpit or lectern and describe their three ways to obey God.

After everyone has finished, say: **It's important to obey God. Even Jesus obeyed God's will. Let's read about how Jesus obeyed God.** Read aloud Matthew 3:13-17. Point out that Jesus was baptized because it was God's will and that Jesus wanted to obey God. Then have the pastor ask:

■ **Why did Jesus want to be baptized?**

■ **How did God show he was pleased with Jesus' obedience?**

■ **Is it hard to obey God all the time? Explain.**

■ **What happens when we don't obey God? What happens when we do?**

CLOSING

Say: **Jesus knew it was good to obey God. And we want to obey God too—even when it's not easy. Let's say a prayer and ask God to help us obey him.** Pray: **Dear God, please help us obey you even when it's difficult. We love you, and obeying your Word is a way to show our love. In Jesus' name, amen.**

MATTHEW
4:2-4

THEME:
God's Word keeps us healthy and happy.

SUMMARY:
In this QUIET REFLECTION, kids discover a surprise message.

PREPARATION: You'll need a Bible, a rock, small bread rolls, a knife, a plate, and small strips of paper with Matthew 4:4 printed on them.

Fold the paper strips with Matthew 4:4 printed on them into tiny squares. Next, cut a one-inch slit in the top of each roll, and insert a folded paper strip into each slit. Push the paper strips deep into the rolls to hide them. Place the rolls on a plate.

Gather the kids into a circle on the floor, and place the rock in the center. Set the plate of rolls behind you. Ask:

■ **When was a time you felt really hungry?**

■ **How does food help someone who's very hungry?**

Say: **Let's read about a time when Jesus was very hungry and rocks were all he could see.**

Read aloud Matthew 4:2-4, then ask:

■ **Who came to tempt Jesus when he was very hungry?**

■ **What did the devil want Jesus to do?**

■ **What did Jesus say about eating bread? about God's Word?**

Say: **I imagine that Jesus was very hungry, but he didn't use his power to turn rocks into bread. Jesus knew that although bread may feed our bodies, God's Word feeds our souls. Jesus knew that knowing God's Word and loving God are even more important than food.** Ask:

■ **How do we learn about God's Word?**

Hand a roll to each child. Say: **Let's ask God's blessing on this bread before we eat it. Bow your heads. Lord, thank you for this bread and for all the food that makes our bodies healthy. Thank you for your words to us in the Bible. Your words are like food; they help us to live in faith and be healthy followers. In Jesus' name, amen.**

Now carefully break open your roll to find a secret message!

MATTHEW
5:14-16

THEME:
Let your light and love for Jesus shine through.

SUMMARY:
In this SERVICE PROJECT, kids sing carols on a summer's evening to benefit others.

PREPARATION: Ask each participant to bring a flashlight and a parent's written permission slip to participate in this activity.

Recruit adult volunteers to drive

or walk with the group. Also determine who the carolers will visit—senior citizens' facilities, hospitals, and nursing homes, for example. You'll also need a Bible and a snack, such as doughnuts and juice, for the group to enjoy afterward.

Gather everyone outside under the twilight sky. Say: **Welcome to an evening of fun! You may wonder why we're caroling by flashlight tonight, so I want to read a passage of Scripture that will give you some clues.**
Read aloud Matthew 5:14-16, then ask:
■ **Whose love makes us shine like a light?**
■ **Why does Jesus want us to spread his love to others?**
■ **How does it feel to spread Jesus' love?**
Say: **Tonight we're going to spread our love by visiting people who need a little cheering up. We'll let our love-light shine by singing special songs to them. We'll pretend it's Christmas in July, and we'll spread some warm Christmas cheer in summer by singing Christmas songs.** Suggest songs such as "Silent Night," "Away in a Manger," "The First Noel," and "Joy to the World."
After you return from singing, provide tasty treats for hungry carolers to enjoy.

MATTHEW
5:21-22

THEME:
We should be careful what we do and say.

SUMMARY:
In this OBJECT LESSON, kids act out arguments and then discuss Jesus' statement about anger.

PREPARATION: You'll need a Bible and a variety of objects that could be the focus of a disagreement—a baseball, a candy bar, a broken piece of jewelry, a toy, a diary, or a remote control for the TV, for example.

Gather children in a group and ask:
■ **When have you been angry with someone or had someone angry with you?**
Have children form pairs, and hand each pair an object that could be the focus of a disagreement. Say: **We often get in fights or disagreements over objects. Look at the object you have, and think of a fight or quarrel that someone might have over this object. Then decide how you can best act out that argument for the rest of the class.**
Circulate and offer help as needed. Call time after five minutes, and invite partners to perform their skits. For extra fun and a great keepsake, have a volunteer videotape the skits. After each skit, ask the following questions:
■ **Would getting mad help this problem? Explain.**

■ **How can this problem be solved without anger?**

After all the pairs have presented their skits, say: **Let's read what the Bible says about anger.** Read aloud Matthew 5:21-22. Ask:

■ **Why is it important to control our anger?**

■ **What happens when someone loses his or her temper?**

■ **How can you control your anger and not get mad at things or people?**

Say: **Sometimes we forget and become angry at other people. What can we do when that happens?** Pause for responses. **Jesus says we should guard against anger unless we want to be punished. It's important to give our anger to God in a prayer and let God take our angry feelings away. Let's pray and ask God to help us control our anger. Dear God, please forgive us for all the times we have spoken angrily and said bad things. Help us give our anger to you. Amen.**

MATTHEW
6:9-13

THEME:
We can pray as Jesus prayed.

SUMMARY:
In this unusual CRAFT project, kids create see-through posters to remind them of the Lord's Prayer.

PREPARATION: You'll need a Bible; newspaper; scissors; white paper; tape; colorful permanent markers; newsprint; and clear plastic vinyl, which is available at most craft and fabric stores.

Cut the vinyl into enough twelve-inch squares for each child to have one. Cover a table with newspaper. If you have children who can read, print the words to the Lord's Prayer on a large sheet of newsprint, and tape the newsprint to the wall.

Gather kids at the table that's covered with newspaper. Ask:

■ **What is prayer?**

■ **How does praying bring us closer to God?**

■ **When do you pray?**

Say: **Prayer is very important. It's a way we talk to God and tell him how we're feeling. We can ask God for help through prayers; we can thank God through prayers; and we can tell God we love him through prayers. Did you know that even Jesus prayed to God? Let's read one of Jesus' prayers to God. In his prayer, Jesus teaches us how to pray.**

Read aloud Matthew 6:9-13. Then ask:

■ **What did Jesus say in his prayer to God?**

Say: **The prayer that Jesus prayed is called the Lord's Prayer. Isn't it beautiful? We can make a special craft to remind us to follow Jesus' example when we pray.**

Place the colored markers on the table. Hand each child a sheet of white paper and a vinyl square. Say: **Today we'll make an unusual see-through poster.** Have children use markers to decorate their see-through posters. Have older children copy the words to the Lord's Prayer on their vinyl squares first and then embellish the edges. Let young children simply create pretty designs on the vinyl; then help them write "amen" in the center of their designs.

When all the posters are finished, let children have an "art show" to display their creations. Demonstrate how the vinyl sticks to clean glass, metal, or plastic surfaces. Encourage children to stick their prayer reminders to a window at home.

MATTHEW
7:7-8

THEME:
God wants us to pray for what we need.

SUMMARY:
In this creative PRAYER activity, children are guided through prayer at three different activity centers.

PREPARATION: You'll need a Bible, three pieces of poster board, markers, scissors, glue sticks, and magazines.

First create three prayer centers by writing a center's title on a piece of poster board. Title one center "Asking," another center "Searching," and the third center "Knocking." Under the Asking poster, place a few magazines, scissors, and a glue stick. Under the Searching poster, place several markers. And under the Knocking poster, place a glue stick, scissors, a few magazines, and several markers.

On the appropriate pieces of poster board, write the following directions:

■ Asking—Choose a picture from a magazine that shows what you or someone you know might need. Glue the picture to this poster, and tell your group why it's important to ask God for what we need.

■ Searching—Write one word on this poster that tells who or how you can ask for what you need. For example, you might write the words "God," "Jesus," or "prayer" on the poster.

■ Knocking—Now think about prayer. Cut out a picture of a person, and glue it to this poster. Or draw a picture of someone praying to show that prayer is a way of asking God to open doors.

Gather the children and ask:
■ **When have you asked God for something in prayer?**
■ **What did you ask for?**
■ **Did you receive what you needed?**
Say: **Today we're going to learn the importance of asking God for what we need. Let's read from the book of Matthew.** Read aloud Matthew 7:7-8. Then say: **God wants us to ask and search and knock on his door for what we need. Knocking on God's door is what we do when we pray.**

Have the children form three groups, and have each group begin at a different prayer center. Have groups follow the directions on the posters. Circulate and offer help to children who can't read or who need additional help. Allow groups to spend five minutes at the first center and then rotate to new centers. After five more minutes, have groups rotate again. After groups are finished with all the prayer centers, look at the posters as a whole group. Encourage children to talk about which words and pictures they chose and why.

Then say: **Jesus taught us to pray to God for what we need. And we can also pray to God for things that other people need. The important thing to remember is that God wants us to ask him and trust him for what we need. Let's pray right now and ask for God's help.** Pray: **Dear God, thank you for hearing our prayers. Please help us remember to ask you for things we need and for things that will help others. In Jesus' name, amen.**

Leave the posters on the wall for everyone to enjoy.

MATTHEW
9:9-12

THEME:
God wants us to help people who are doing wrong things.

SUMMARY:
In this active DEVOTION, kids decide whether to eat with "good people" or "bad people" and then learn who Jesus chose to eat with.

PREPARATION: For this activity, you'll need a Bible; two sheets of paper; a marker; two tables; and a simple snack, such as crackers and cheese, served on two paper plates. Make enough snacks for each child in the class plus a few extras.

On one sheet of paper write, "Welcome, Good People"; on the other sheet, write, "Welcome, Bad People." Place a welcome sign on each table along with one plate of prepared snacks.

EXPERIENCE
Begin by welcoming children and inviting them to choose a table to sit at. Let children sit wherever they choose. If you have nonreaders, read the table signs for them.

Encourage everyone to enjoy the treats. As children eat, talk about why they chose to sit at that particular table. Ask questions such as, "Why would anyone want to sit at a table with people who do bad things?" and "Who needs more love and understanding: someone who loves God or someone who doesn't know God yet?"

After a few moments, say: **The table signs lead us to an interesting Bible story. As you finish your snacks, I'll read from the book of Matthew.** Read aloud Matthew 9:9-12.

RESPONSE
Close the Bible and ask:
■ **If Jesus were here right now, where do you think he'd sit? Why?**
Say: **When Jesus ate with robbers, tax collectors, and other sinners, people were surprised. They thought Jesus shouldn't love those people.** Ask:
■ **Why do you think Jesus ate with those people?**
■ **Do you think Jesus was right to eat with those people? Explain.**

■ **How would you feel if no one liked you but then Jesus sat down to eat with you?**

Say: **Jesus ate with sinners because he loved them. Jesus wanted to help people learn to do what's right. Let's see how to help others do the right things.** Ask:

■ **How can you help a classmate who calls other people mean names?**

■ **How can you help a friend who stole something from a store?**

■ **How can you help your best friend who lied to his parents?**

CLOSING

Close by saying: **Jesus wants us to do the right things. And he knows that people who do wrong things need our help. That's why Jesus chose to eat with people who needed help. We can remember Jesus' choice by choosing to help others who are mixed up or doing wrong things.**

MATTHEW
10:32-33

THEME:
    Jesus wants us to tell others that we're Christians.

SUMMARY:
    In this LEARNING GAME, children have the chance to tell others of their faith.

PREPARATION: You'll need a Bible, paper, tape, a red marker, a paper bag, a cassette player, a cassette tape of lively music, and a small trinket or prize for each child. Prizes might include balloons, party horns, stickers, erasers, boxes of raisins, or small pocket Bibles.

Tape sheets of paper to the floor in a large circle. Be sure the sheets are two feet apart. Draw a heart shape on one of the sheets. Place the prizes in a bag, then set them in the center of the circle.

Say: **We're going to play a game for people who believe in Jesus. Find a sheet of paper to stand on, then listen as I read what Jesus said about believing in him.** Read aloud Matthew 10:32-33.

Say: **Jesus said that if we believe in him, we can stand before others and tell them about our faith. We want others to know we love and follow Jesus. In the Follower's Game, you'll have a chance to tell others you believe in Jesus. When the music starts, hop from paper to paper around the circle. When the music stops, freeze on a sheet of paper. The person on or closest to the heart will go to the center of the circle. That person may say aloud, "I love Jesus" or "I follow Jesus" or "I'm a Christian." Then he or she may choose a treat from the treat bag and may stay in the center of the circle.**

Play the music in intervals of several seconds until all the children have had a chance to tell the others about their faith.

After everyone is in the center of the circle and has a treat, ask:

■ **Who do we believe in, love, and follow?**

Lead everyone in a final cheer, saying, "I'm Jesus' follower! Yea!"

MATTHEW
11:28-30

THEME:
We can trust Jesus to help us with our problems.

SUMMARY:
In this MUSIC IDEA, children enjoy an action song as they learn that Jesus carries our burdens.

PREPARATION: For this activity, you'll need a Bible; newspaper; and a large, plastic garbage bag.

Hand each child a sheet of newspaper, and have kids get with partners. Say: **Tell your partner about a time you felt afraid or worried, and then crumple your paper.** Allow two minutes for partners to share. Then say: **Fears and worries can feel like a heavy load. Let's see what the Bible says about heavy loads and who can make them lighter.**

Read aloud Matthew 11:28-30. Ask:

■ **Who can help lighten our loads?**

■ **How will we feel when we come to Jesus for his help?**

Say: **We all have troubles and worries, but Jesus wants us to know that he's always ready to help. Jesus wants to lighten our heavy loads. Let's make a pre-**tend **load to carry; then we'll sing a song as we try to carry our heavy load.**

Have children stand in a circle and pass the plastic bag from person to person. Have each child say, "I'll give my troubles to Jesus" as he or she drops a paper wad into the bag. When the bag is filled, sing the following song to the tune of "Row, Row, Row Your Boat" as you continue passing the bag around the circle.

Come, come, come to him *(make beckoning motions with your arms)*
When your load's not light. *(Sit on your heels.)*
Jesus wants to lift you up *(cover your heart and slowly stand)*
And make your heart feel bright. *(Put your hands in the air and wiggle your fingers.)*

Lean, lean, lean on him *(lean to one side, then to the other)*
When you have a frown. *(Raise arms out from sides.)*
Jesus wants to give you love *(cover your heart with your hand)*
When you're feeling down. *(Keep covering your heart and sit in place.)*

Older children may enjoy singing this action song as a round. If you choose to sing the song this way, stop passing the plastic bag around the circle.

MATTHEW
12:33-37

THEME:
God wants us to say good things.

SUMMARY:
In this PARTY idea, children play a variety of fun games as they learn the value of saying good things.

PREPARATION: Make photocopies of the party invitations on page 22, and be sure each child receives one.

For party games, you'll need an apple or orange for each child, a Bible, and two bananas.

For party treats, let children form an assembly line to create a fruity pizza. You'll need a pizza pan, softened cream cheese, plastic knives, a variety of fresh or canned fruits, a package of refrigerated sugar-cookie dough, and access to an oven. If you don't have an oven, bake the

sugar-cookie crust prior to the party.

You may wish to jazz up your party motif by inviting children to create fruity hats to wear. Simply provide colorful paper and tape, and have children design "banana beanies," "berry berets," or "apple caps" to wear.

Have children form a large circle. Say: **Welcome to our Good Fruit Party. Today we'll learn how we can be God's good fruit by speaking good things to one another.** Ask:

■ **What are nice things we can say to one another?**

Lead children in making comments such as "You're a friendly person," "You help others," "I like your smile," or "You love Jesus and it shows!"

Put a bag full of apples or oranges in the center of the floor. Say: **It's nice to say good things, and it can be fun, too. Let's play a fun game called the Banana-Phone Game. I'll put two "banana-phones" in the center of the floor. Then we'll form two groups and give each person a number to remember.** Place two bananas in the center of the floor for the banana-phones. Then help children count off so each group has a number one, a number two, and so on. Then say: **I'll call out two numbers. People with those numbers must hop to the banana-phones and pick one up. Talking into them like telephones, tell the person "on the other end" of the phone one good thing such as "You're fun to be with." After both messages have been spoken, choose an apple or orange, then sit in your place in** the circle. Don't eat your fruit yet, though.

Play the game until everyone is sitting and holding an apple or orange. Then say: **Your banana-phone messages were all good things to say. Jesus wants us to know that what we say shows what's in our hearts. Let's listen to what Jesus said about saying nice things.** Read aloud Matthew 12:33-37. Ask:

■ **If someone says good things, what is that person's heart like? If someone says bad things, what is that person's heart like?**

■ **Why is it important to say good things?**

■ **How can we be God's good fruit?**

Say: **When we say good things,** it shows that we have good things inside. Now let's stand up and play another good-fruit game. You'll need the fruit you're holding to play. I'll give you special directions to follow, so listen carefully.

Toss your fruit in the air and catch it. Say something good about yourself. Pause for responses.

Find a partner, and toss your fruit to that person. Pause. **Now say something good about your partner.** Pause for responses.

Toss your fruit back to each other and say something good about a special friend you have. Pause.

Now toss your fruit in the air again and catch it. Say something good about God. Pause for

We're "PLUM" pleased to invite you to a party! "ORANGE" you excited? We'll have "GRAPE" fun— hope to see you there!

When: _____

Where: _____

From: _____

P.S. Bring a friend so you can be a "PEAR."

responses, then ask children to set their fruit aside.

Set out the fruit-pizza items in the following order: pizza pan, sugar-cookie dough, softened cream cheese, plastic knives, and fruit. Have several children flatten the cookie dough in the pizza pan. Bake the dough for seven to nine minutes in a 350-degree oven. As the crust bakes, have several children wash and cut the fruit into slices and small chunks.

After the crust has cooled, let a few children spread softened cream cheese on top. Then have the rest of the children top the pizza with a variety of fresh fruit.

MATTHEW
13:18-23

THEME:
We can let God's Word grow within us.

SUMMARY:
On this field TRIP, children plant flower seeds and learn how they can let God's Word grow deeply in their hearts.

PREPARATION: Choose a place to plant flower seeds—the church grounds, a friend's yard, or a near-by park, for example. You'll need permission to plant your flowers. With the parable of the sower and seeds in mind, check out your chosen location to make sure there's a road, a rocky area, a weedy spot, and a place with good soil.

Obtain written permission from parents or caregivers for the children to travel if you're going off-grounds. Recruit drivers or extra helpers if you need them. If you cannot travel with the children, provide several large pots with soil to plant the seeds in your classroom.

You'll need a Bible, a watering can, plastic spoons, and fast-growing flower seeds such as marigolds, morning glorys, or zinnias.

When you arrive at your planting destination, show children the flower seeds and ask:

■ **What do seeds need to grow?**

■ **Where is the best place to plant seeds?**

■ **Are there any places where seeds just can't grow?**

Say: **We're going to plant flower seeds today, but we need to find just the right spot so they'll grow into beautiful, full flowers. Follow me.**

Visit the road, the rocky ground, the weedy area, and the place with good soil. Each time you show a possible planting place, ask:

■ **Is this a good place to plant our seeds? Why or why not?**

When children "discover" the good soil, have them sit down. Open the packages of flower seeds, and hand a seed to each child. Say: **Jesus knew about so many things, didn't he? He also knew about planting seeds. Let's hear what Jesus had to say about the best place to plant seeds. Hold your seeds carefully as you listen to the story.** Read aloud Matthew 13:18-23, then ask:

■ **In Jesus' story, the seed is like God's Word. What are the** different types of ground in the story like? Guide children to realize that the types of ground represent the way different types of people receive God's Word.

■ What kind of ground do we want to be?

■ When God's Word is planted in us, how do we care for it? Encourage children to name such ways as going to church, praying, learning about God, reading the Bible, and being kind to others.

Hand each child several more seeds and a plastic spoon. Invite children to plant their seeds in the "good soil." Cover the seeds with soil, then water them carefully.

After the seeds have been planted, form a circle around the planted seeds and hold hands. Pray: **Dear God, please help us be good soil so your Word can grow deep within us. In Jesus' name we pray, amen.**

Make a point to water the seeds regularly until the plants are hardy. Then arrange for the children to return to see the flowers.

MATTHEW
16:15-18

THEME:
Each of us is an important part of the church.

SUMMARY:
In this SERVICE PROJECT, children cooperatively build a "church" as they learn what it means to be an active part of the church congregation.

PREPARATION: You'll need a Bible, two buttered nine-by-thirteen-inch pans, two boxes of crisp-rice cereal, two bags of miniature marshmallows, two large tubes of prepared frosting, a stick of butter, a box of graham crackers, a large serving tray, an ice-cream sugar cone, a mixing spoon, a spatula, a knife, a stove- or microwave-proof pan, and access to a stove or microwave. You may also wish to provide optional decorations such as raisins, tiny cinnamon candies, gum drops, rope licorice, and peanuts.

Before class, prepare two pans of crisp-rice cereal treats by melting a stick of butter with two bags of marshmallows, then by gently stirring in two boxes of crisp-rice cereal. Spread the mixture into the two buttered pans, and cut the cereal treats into eighty one-inch "bricks." Remove the cereal bricks from the pans. If your church will need many more or less than eighty one-inch bricks, adjust the recipe accordingly.

Set out the cereal bricks; graham crackers; frosting; sugar cone; serving tray; and any optional, decorative items.

Gather the children and ask: ■ Who are some people who help at our church? Encourage children to name the pastor, music leader, secretary, Sunday school teachers, and other people who are actively involved.

Say: **The Christian church is named for Jesus Christ. Jesus started the church, but he wanted other people to help start many, many churches all over the world. Listen to the story of how the church began.** Read

aloud Matthew 16:15-18, then ask:
■ **How did Peter know that Jesus was God's Son?**
■ **The name Peter means "rock," so Jesus named Peter a "rock." Why would it be good to build a church on a rock?**
■ **Why is it important to help at church?**
■ **How can we all be active helpers at church?**

Say: **Jesus knew he could count on Peter to begin building the church, but Jesus needs us to be active members of church, too. Today we're going to help by making a special dessert for everyone in church to enjoy. We'll pretend to be Peter and build the church from tasty building materials.**

Have children wash their hands. Help the children follow the directions below to build the edible church.

Step 1: Make four church "walls," each four cereal bricks high and four bricks long. Squirt frosting "mortar" between each layer of bricks and around the base of the church.

Step 2: Break a graham cracker in half, then use frosting to attach

the halves to the front of the church as double doors. Add raisin or peanut door handles if you desire.

Step 3: Squirt frosting mortar along the top edge of the bricks, and attach graham crackers for the roof. You may need to overlap crackers and use frosting to hold them in place.

Step 4: Attach a sugar-cone "steeple" to the roof with frosting. Use frosting to add a licorice cross if you desire.

Step 5: Use frosting to attach raisins, peanuts, gumdrops, and tiny cinnamon candies as decorations for the church if you desire.

Arrange for the children to serve the treat during a special fellowship time after worship. Encourage children to greet each church member and thank them for being part of the church.

MATTHEW
18:10-14

THEME:
God looks for us and brings us back if we wander from him.

SUMMARY:
In this MUSIC IDEA, young children have fun learning about the parable of the lost sheep and singing an action song.

PREPARATION: You'll need a Bible.

Greet children and ask:
■ **Have any of you ever gotten lost or separated from**

your family? Tell about your experience.

■ How did it feel to be lost?

■ Who found you? What happened when you were found?

Say: **Your family doesn't want you to stray away from their love and safety and care. In the same way, Jesus doesn't want us to stray from him or the love and care of our church family.** Let's hear a special story Jesus told about a lost sheep and the shepherd who searched to find it. You can help tell the story. When you hear the word "sheep," gently say "baaa." Demonstrate how to sound like a sheep. Let children practice their sound effect for a moment, then read aloud Matthew 18:10-14. Ask:

■ Why do you think the shepherd was worried about his sheep?

■ How long will a good shepherd look for his lost sheep?

■ How did the shepherd feel when the lost sheep was found?

Say: **God doesn't want you to become lost from his love. God loves you and wants grown-ups like me and the people in our church to help keep you close to God. We can be like good shepherds and keep God's lambs close to him.**

Let's sing a fun song to remind us that God looks for us if we're lost. I'll choose two people to be Shepherds. The rest of you will be Sheep. Shepherds can hide their eyes as the Sheep hide. Then we'll sing a song while the Shepherds look for the Sheep. Sheep, when a Shepherd finds you, he or she will lead you to the center of the room. Stay there until all the Sheep have been found.

Have the Shepherds cover their eyes while the Sheep hide around the room. Then have the class sing the following song to the tune of "London Bridge." As the class sings, have the Shepherds find the hidden Sheep and then gently guide the Sheep to the center of the room.

> **God will find me if I'm lost,**
> **If I'm lost,**
> **If I'm lost.**
> **God will find me if I'm lost.**
> **He loves and cares for me.**
>
> **I'm a sheep in Jesus' flock,**
> **Jesus' flock,**
> **Jesus' flock.**
> **I'm a sheep in Jesus' flock.**
> **He loves and cares for me.**

Play and sing until each child has been a Shepherd.

MATTHEW 20:1-16

THEME:

When we serve God, we'll be first in his kingdom.

SUMMARY:

In this OBJECT LESSON, children experience an adapted version of the parable of the workers.

PREPARATION: For this activity, you'll need a Bible; a bucket of water; newspaper; sponges; scissors; a variety of storybooks or jigsaw puzzles; and a small treat—such as a cookie, wrapped candy, or box of raisins—for each child. Since the treats will be used as "pay," gold-foil-wrapped chocolate coins work very well.

Before class, cut sponges into two-inch pieces. Prepare a sponge for each child. Set the bucket of water on newspaper in one corner of the room. Decide which items in the room the children can wash—tables, chairs, counter tops, windows, the door, or the floorboards, for example.

Have the children form three groups, and give each group several books or a puzzle. Encourage group members to work together to read or put puzzles together.

Approach one group and whisper: **I'd like to hire you to wash the tables. I'll pay you well for your work.** Hand each child in this group a sponge, and help the children get started washing the tables.

After a few moments, address another group. Say: **I'd like to hire you to wash the chairs. I'll pay you well for your work.** Hand each child in this group a sponge, and help the children get started washing the chairs. Instruct the others to keep washing the tables.

Address the last group of children. Say: **I'd like to hire you to wipe off the wastebasket. I'll pay you well for your hard work.** Hand each child in this group a sponge, and help the children get started washing the wastebasket. Have the other groups continue to clean their items.

After a few moments, say: **It's time to stop your work. All workers, come receive your pay.** Bring out the treats. Say: **All of you who began to work last, come forward.** Give each child in the group a treat. **Workers I hired second, come get your pay.** Give each child in the group a treat. **Now the workers I hired first, collect your fair pay.** Hand each child in the group a treat. Then ask:
■ **Who worked the longest?**
■ **Who received the most pay?**
■ **Was your payment fair? Explain.**
■ **Was your work worth more than someone else's work?**

Say: **Sometimes we think that if we work very hard, we should get more in return. And if we don't receive more, we often feel that we're in last place. But God has a different way of paying us. As you nibble your treats, let's find out what the Bible says about being first and last with God.**

Read aloud Matthew 20:1-16. Then say: **The story tells us that whoever has last place now will be first in the future. It may be hard work to serve God now, and we may not feel that we're getting paid for our work. But God wants us to know that he has wonderful things for us in heaven and that we'll be paid greatly for serving him now.**

MATTHEW
21:6-11

THEME:
We can praise Jesus and welcome him into our lives.

SUMMARY:
In this colorful parade PARTY, children praise Jesus and celebrate his triumphal entry into Jerusalem.

PREPARATION: You'll need a Bible, paper cups, plastic drinking straws, tape, green and brown crepe paper, a musical cassette tape, and a cassette player. You'll also need a bag of large marshmallows, a bowl of water, and a bowl of rainbow candy sprinkles to make special party treats called praise poppers.

Before class, tape a brown crepe paper path along the floor. Let the path wind around the entire room and end up at a snack table. On the table, set out drinking straws, marshmallows, the bowl of water, and the bowl of candy sprinkles.

As children arrive, give them paper cups, and invite them to tape green crepe paper streamers to their cups for palm fronds. As children work, say: **I hear there's a parade coming! We'll make-believe we're part of the special parade. Let's walk along this path and wave our pretend palm branches. As we walk along, we'll shout, "Hosanna, hosanna! Praise to God!"** Turn on the music, and lead the children in a parade around the room. Stay on the paper path, and encourage children to wave their paper-cup palm branches and say, "Hosanna! Praise to God!"

When you come to the end of the path, have children sit down. Say: **Do you know who this special parade is for? Let's read in the Bible to find out who a special parade in Jerusalem was for.** Read aloud Matthew 21:6-11. Then ask:

■ **Who was this parade for?**
■ **Why did people praise God?**

Say: **The parade was to celebrate Jesus' arrival, and people praised him by waving palm branches and by placing their coats along the path. We can have a special celebration too. Let's make praise poppers to remind us to praise God for his Son every day.**

Show children how to poke a drinking straw down through the bottom of a paper cup, then stick two marshmallows on the top of the straw. After the children have finished, let them carefully dip their marshmallows in water and then roll them in the candy sprinkles. Before children eat their treats, have them push their praise poppers up and down and say, "Hosanna! Praise to God!"

MATTHEW
22:34-40

THEME:
Jesus teaches us to love God and to love each other.

SUMMARY:
In this AFFIRMATION ACTIVITY, children have a friendly "shouting match" to learn Jesus' two love commands.

PREPARATION: You'll need a Bible.

This activity gives children a chance to shout a rousing cheer. If you think the noise may disturb others, consider going outdoors or to an isolated area.

Form two groups: Group A and Group B. Ask each group to huddle, explaining that each will soon receive a special message from Jesus.

In a whisper, say to Group A: **Your message is, "Love God with all your heart, soul, and mind."** **Now whisper it back to me.** Pause for the response. **Keep practicing your message until we begin.**

Go to Group B and whisper: **Your message is, "Love your neighbor as you love yourself." Whisper the message back to me.** Pause for the response. **Keep practicing your message until we begin.**

After a few moments, have both groups stand, facing each other, about seven feet apart.

Say: **Group A, tell Group B your message.** Pause for Group A to repeat its message. **Now Group B, tell Group A your message.** Go

back and forth, repeating the messages and getting a bit louder each round. Continue until each group ends with one last, rousing retort.

Have the children sit down to rest their "victory voices." Say: **You remembered your special messages very well. Do you know where these messages come from? Let's take a look in the Bible.** Read aloud Matthew 22:34-40. Then talk about the importance of loving God and loving others. End with a challenge to see if Group A can repeat Group B's message and vice versa.

MATTHEW
25:1-13

THEME:
We want to be ready for Jesus.

SUMMARY:
In this fast-paced LEARNING GAME, children try to be the first ones "ready" as they layer on dress-up clothes and learn the parable of the ten bridesmaids.

PREPARATION: You'll need a Bible and a generous amount of adult-sized shirts, vests, sports jackets, dresses, sweaters, neckties, belts, jewelry, and gloves. You'll also need graham crackers and apple juice.

Separate the dress-up items into two equal piles. Have children form two groups. Say: **We're going to a pretend party. To be** ready, your group must put on every article of clothing in your pile. Nothing can be left. When your group is ready say, "We're ready for Jesus!" Get ready, set, go!

When the race is over, say: **You were fast and got ready in a hurry. You can all sit down, and we'll have a little party while we listen to a special story Jesus told.**

Pass out graham crackers and apple juice. Read aloud Matthew 25:1-13. Then ask:

■ **Do we know when Jesus will come back to us on earth?**

■ **Why is it important to be ready for Jesus?**

Say: **Jesus told this story of the ten bridesmaids to help us realize that we need to be wise and ready for his return.** Ask:

■ **How can we get ready for Jesus?** Encourage children to list things such as praying, reading the Bible, learning about Jesus, and loving others.

Close with a prayer. Pray: **Dear God, thank you for Jesus. Please help us be ready for Jesus. Amen.** Have a reverse race to put the clothes back in piles.

MATTHEW
26:26-28

THEME:
Jesus wants us to remember and accept his forgiveness.

SUMMARY:
In this QUIET REFLECTION, children learn about the Last Supper and how Jesus wants us to have his forgiveness.

PREPARATION: You'll need a Bible.

Begin by saying: **Give me a thumbs up because you're here today.** Pause. **Now give me a thumbs down if you've ever heard the word "sin."** Pause, then ask:

■ **What does the word "sin" mean?** Lead children to realize that sin is when we do things that God tells us are wrong.

■ **Who has sinned?** Point out that we've all sinned. You may wish to read aloud Romans 3:23.

Say: **When we sin, we go away from God; we can't be God's friends. But Jesus offers us forgiveness so we can be God's friends again. I'm going to read the story of Jesus' Last Supper. Whenever you hear the word "sin," give a thumbs down. When you hear the word "forgive," give a thumbs up.** Read aloud Matthew 26:26-28.

Say: **Jesus told his followers that his death would provide forgiveness and that we could live as God's friends again. Let's pray and ask God to forgive us** for the wrong things we've done. This prayer is just between you and God. It's a fill-in-the-blank prayer. Listen to what I say, and when I'm silent, fill in the blanks with your own thoughts. Have children close their eyes.

Pray: **Dear God, I know that I do wrong things sometimes. Let me tell you about the mistakes I made this week. While at school, I** (pause). **I hurt my friend's feelings when I** (pause). **At home, I shouldn't have** (pause). **And I know I shouldn't have said** (pause). **I'm sorry for the wrong things I've done, and I ask for your forgiveness, God. I love you. In Jesus' name, amen.**

MATTHEW
26:36-41

THEME:
Jesus wants us to resist temptation.

SUMMARY:
In this OBJECT LESSON, children learn that Jesus' followers were tempted to sleep as he prayed.

PREPARATION: For this activity, you'll need a Bible and one noise-maker for each child. Kazoos are great fun and are available at most party-supply stores.

Gather children in a circle on the floor, and place the noise-makers in the center. Invite the children to look at the noisemakers and touch them but to not make noise with them. After a few moments, ask:

■ **How many of you would like to make noise with the noisemakers?**

■ **What is temptation?**

■ **Is it hard to resist the temptation of making noise?**

Say: **Sometimes we're very tempted to do just what we know we shouldn't do. But Jesus wants us to fight temptation and do what's right. Let's listen to a Bible story about a time Jesus' followers gave in to temptation.** Read aloud Matthew 26:36-41. Ask:

■ **What couldn't Jesus' followers resist?**

■ **What had Jesus asked his followers to do?**

■ **How do you think Jesus' friends felt when Jesus woke them?**

■ **What did Jesus mean when he said, "The spirit wants to do what is right, but the body is weak?"** Help the children understand that although our hearts want to do the right things, our bodies often want to do the wrong things—and often win.

Say: **Sometimes we're tempted to do things that we know are wrong.** Ask:

■ **Who can tell about a time you or someone you knew was tempted?**

■ **What did you do?**

Say: **Jesus told his followers to pray for strength against temptation. That's a good thing to do when we're tempted toward wrong things. Let's bow our heads and ask God to help** us resist temptation.

Pray: **Dear Lord, every day we're tempted to do wrong things. We have to choose between right and wrong. Please help us be strong and fight against temptation. In Jesus' name, amen.**

Invite the kids to wake up any "sleepy followers" by making a joyful noise with the noisemakers. If the noisemakers can carry a tune or keep a beat, use them to sing a familiar song like "Amen," "Do, Lord," or "Jesus Loves Me."

MATTHEW 27:57-60

THEME:
We can be faithful to Jesus.

SUMMARY:
In this CRAFT activity, children sculpt special paperweights to help them remember the story of one follower's faithfulness to Jesus.

PREPARATION: You'll need a Bible and modeling dough or self-hardening clay.

Before class, prepare a batch of modeling dough using the following recipe.

Combine one cup of flour, one-fourth cup of salt, two tablespoons of cream of tartar, one cup of water, one tablespoon of oil, and two teaspoons of food coloring in a saucepan. Cook over medium heat, stirring often. After three to five minutes, a sticky ball of dough will form. Turn the ball out on a lightly floured surface. Let the dough cool slightly, then knead the dough until it's pliable. Store modeling dough in an airtight container.

Gather the children, then ask:
■ **What does it mean to be faithful?**

■ **When have you been faithful to someone or had someone be faithful to you?**

■ **Why do we want to be faithful to Jesus?**

Say: **Today we're going to learn about a time one of Jesus' friends was faithful to him. You can help tell the story. Every time you hear the name "Jesus," place your hand over your heart to show that we want to be faithful to Jesus.** Read aloud Matthew 27:57-60. After reading, ask:

■ **Why did Joseph go to Pilate?**

■ **What did Joseph do for Jesus?**

■ **How was providing a tomb for Jesus being faithful to him?**

Say: **Joseph was one of Jesus' followers. But he was also Jesus' friend. Joseph knew that friends are faithful to each other, and we know that Jesus is a friend we want to be faithful to.** Ask:

■ **How can we show our faithfulness to Jesus?** Encourage children to name ways such as praying, learning about Jesus, telling others about Jesus, and loving others as Jesus loves us.

Say: **To help us remember to be faithful to Jesus, we'll pretend to be sculptors and sculpt a figure from the story of Joseph and the tomb. You may wish to sculpt the tomb or a figure of Joseph or even the angel who rolled the stone away from the tomb on Easter morning. When the sculptures are dry, they'll be great paperweights!**

As the kids work, discuss Joseph's faithfulness to Jesus even after Jesus' death. Point out that when we're faithful to Jesus, it shows our great love for him.

MATTHEW 28:1-10

THEME:

We can celebrate that Jesus is alive.

SUMMARY:

In this QUIET REFLECTION, children will express joy that Jesus is alive.

PREPARATION: You'll need a Bible, clear plastic cups (available in party stores), small household candles, matches, and scissors.

Before this activity, you'll need to prepare a candleholder for each child. Carefully use scissors to poke a hole through the bottom of each plastic cup. The hole should be slightly smaller than the diameter of a candle. Slide a candle through the hole so the bottom of the candle makes a "handle" and the top is midway inside the cup. Be sure the candle is held tightly in the plastic cup and cannot slide through the hole.

Darken the room slightly, and place the cups and candles behind you. Gather children in a circle on the floor. Say: **I have a wonderful story to read to you. It's a story of sadness and darkness, like our room is now. But we'll find out how that dark sadness turned to beautiful, light joy.** Read aloud Matthew 28:1-10. After reading, ask:

■ **Why were Jesus' friends so sad?**

■ **Do you think Jesus' friends thought they'd ever be happy again? Explain.**

■ **How do you think Jesus' friends felt when they realized Jesus was alive?**

Say: **Stand up and find a partner. You can act out the motions in a special poem I'd like to read to you.** Read the following poem, and encourage children to create their own motions to act out the words.

The women walked to Jesus' tomb
Feeling sad and full of gloom.

Then all of a sudden, the friends looked down;
They felt an earthquake shake the ground!
Then an angel bright as lightning shone
And with God's power, rolled the stone.
The angel said, "Please don't fear,
Jesus is alive—he's no longer here!
Go tell his friends in Galilee,
Jesus will go there for them to see."
The women were happy for what had occurred,
So they ran to tell all they had heard.
But on the way home, what happened then?
They met Jesus and worshiped him.

Pass out the candles in the plastic cups. Instruct the children to hold the candles by the handles and to leave them in the cups. Say: **When Jesus was dead, the world was dark and sad. But when the angel of light came and told Mary and her friends that Jesus was alive, the world became light! We'll light these candles to celebrate the joy we have knowing that Jesus is alive. When the candles are lit, we'll say a quiet prayer and then blow out the candles. After your candle is lit, hold it away from you, and be careful not to tip the candle.**
Light your candle, then use it to light each child's candle. When everyone's candle is lit, say: **Let's have a moment of silence as** you quietly tell God how glad you are that Jesus is alive. Pause for a few moments, then say: **Let's pray. Dear God, we know there was sadness when Jesus died on the cross for us. But we have wonderful joy now because we know that Jesus is alive. Thank you for sending Jesus to love us. We love Jesus too. Amen.** Have children gently blow out their candles; then collect the candles and cups.

MATTHEW 28:18-20

THEME:
We can tell others about Jesus.

SUMMARY:
Use this SKIT to teach kids the importance of telling others about Jesus.

AND NOW, A WORD FROM OUR SPONSOR

SCENE: Several children are playing in a park.

PROPS: You'll need a hand-held video game or small box, a bench or several chairs pushed together, a book, a Walkman radio or small box with headphones, a baseball, and baseball caps.

CHARACTERS:
Narrator (any age or gender)
Patrick (any age, dressed casually)
Toby (tough-looking boy, wearing

his cap backward and playing a hand-held video game)

Lisa (any age, listening to a Walkman with headphones and holding a book)

Jamel (any age, dressed casually, holding a baseball)

Isaac (any age, wearing a baseball cap)

The Stranger (a man, dressed in jeans and a Christian T-shirt)

SCRIPT

(Narrator reads Matthew 28:18-20 from offstage, then kids enter. Jamel and Isaac start playing catch. Lisa sits on a bench, reading and listening to a Walkman. Toby sits on the ground, playing a video game. Patrick enters and approaches Toby.)

Patrick: Hi, Toby. How's it going?

Toby: Awesome, man! I've got a higher score on "Mutant Lizards From Saturn" than I've ever had before. This is so cool!

Patrick: I was wondering . . . if you're not busy this weekend, maybe you'd like to go to Sunday school with me. It's really fun, and we're learning about—

Toby: *(Glancing away from his game for a moment)* You mean church? I . . . *(glancing back at his game)* . . . hey, wait! I just lost my game! My high score disappeared! Thanks a lot, Patrick! *(Walks away, calling over his shoulder)* And no, I don't want to go to church with you!

Patrick: *(Sighs and shakes his head.)* This isn't going to be easy. *(Approaches Lisa.)* Hello, Lisa, what'cha doin'?

(Lisa doesn't hear. She bobs her head to the music on her Walkman and reads her book.)

Patrick: *(Leans down.)* Lisa? Lisa!

Lisa: *(Lifts the headphones)* Huh? Did you say something, Patrick?

Patrick: Yeah, I just wanted to ask you if you want to–

(Lisa puts the headphones back on and turns back to her book.)

Patrick: *(Sighs.)* Never mind. *(Turns attention to Jamel and Isaac.)* Hey guys, what's up?

Jamel: Not much. Wanna play catch?

Isaac: Yeah, you could use the practice!

Patrick: *(Smiles.)* I know, last week's game was a disaster. Um, this weekend my church is having a softball game. Maybe you guys would like to play with us.

Jamel: Softball?

Isaac: Church?

Patrick: I mean, you could go to Sunday school first, then we could play in the softball game.

Isaac: Naw, I don't believe in that God stuff. It's too weird!

Jamel: Yeah, and anyway, we've got practice . . . but I guess you wouldn't remember that!

(Isaac and Jamal laugh and then run offstage. Patrick sighs and sits on the bench beside Lisa. Lisa eyes him, then leaves the stage. The Stranger approaches and sits next to Patrick.)

Patrick: *(Mumbling to himself)* I'll never get this right. I'm no good.

The Stranger: Hi. What's the problem?

Patrick: Aw . . . nothing you'd be interested in. Nobody else is.

The Stranger: Give me a try. You might be surprised.

Patrick: *(Sighs.)* Well, I've been trying to invite my friends to church so they can learn about Jesus. But they don't want to come.

The Stranger: *(Nods.)* I know what you mean. I've had trouble passing on the good news too.

Patrick: You have?

The Stranger: Sure. I tried everything! Teaching them, healing them, showing them miracles. Even calmed a storm or two. *(Sadly shakes his head.)* But some people still didn't listen.

Patrick: *(Looks offstage, where others have left.)* Yeah, I know what that's like.

The Stranger: *(Quietly)* Even death on a cross didn't get everyone's attention. Some people don't want to hear what you've got to say. Even though it's the best news they'll ever hear.

Patrick: *(Suddenly looks at The Stranger.)* Death on a...? Miracles? Storms? That means you're...

The Stranger: *(Stands up to leave and pats Patrick's shoulder.)* Keep trying, Patrick. Even though they don't want to listen, they still need to hear the good news. Don't ever stop telling it. *(The Stranger exits.)*

(Lisa comes bopping through, still listening to the Walkman on headphones. Patrick hesitates, then approaches her.)

Patrick: *(Touches her shoulder.)* Lisa?

Lisa: *(Sighs, turns off the Walkman.)* What, Patrick?

Patrick: Lisa, I...I want to invite you to my Sunday school class. *(The two walk offstage together.)* You see, we're learning about Jesus' miracles, and I think you'd really learn a lot from them. I sure have...

If you use this skit as a discussion starter, here are possible questions:

■ **What makes it hard to tell people about Jesus?**

■ **How can you tell others about Jesus?**

■ **What's the most important thing you could tell someone about Jesus? Why is that an important thing to tell?**

■ **Who can you tell about Jesus?**

MARK

"This is a voice of one who calls out in the desert: 'Prepare the way for the Lord. Make the road straight for him.' "

Mark 1:3

MARK
1:1-8

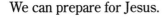

THEME:
We can prepare for Jesus.

SUMMARY:
In this OBJECT LESSON, the children learn why it's important to "make the road straight" for the Lord.

PREPARATION: You'll need a Bible and a long rope.

Make a path in your room with a long rope. Put lots of bends, twists, and curves in the path. If you teach older children, you may want to use more than one rope.

Have the children take off their shoes and walk on the "tightrope." When the first child is several feet along the path, have the next child begin.

After everyone has walked the path, straighten the rope, and have the children walk along the path again. Then gather the children and ask:

■ **Was it easier to walk along the crooked path or the straight path? Explain.**

Say: **The Bible talks about making a crooked path straight. Let's read what it says.** Have the children take turns reading Mark 1:1-8. Ask:

■ **What is the road John is talking about?**

■ **What do you think made the road crooked?**

■ Why did John ask the people to straighten the road?

■ How can we straighten the road today?

Say: **To straighten the road for Jesus means to get ready for his coming. We can get ready for Jesus by looking at our lives and by getting rid of the things that keep us from following Jesus. Then we'll be able to welcome Jesus with our whole hearts.**

If you have time, make a twisted path again, and let the children run a rope relay. Close with a prayer asking God for help in preparing our hearts for Jesus.

MARK
1:14-18

THEME:

Jesus wants us to be fishers of men.

SUMMARY:

For this CRAFT, the children make decorative fish windsocks that remind them to share the good news about Jesus.

PREPARATION: You'll need a Bible, rulers, and plastic lids from coffee cans or margarine tubs. You'll also need large pieces of sturdy white paper, glue, scissors, string or yarn, and markers or crayons.

Ask a volunteer to read Mark 1:14-18 from the Bible. Then say: **Jesus told Simon and** Andrew that they could be fishers of men. We can bring people to Jesus, too, by being fishers of men. Let's make a craft that reminds us to be fishers of men.

Give each child a plastic lid and two pieces of white paper. Have each child set his or her lid in a corner of a piece of paper and measure the diameter of the lid. Help younger children fold their papers to mark the top and bottom of the circles to see how tall their lids are.

Have each child draw a large fish with an open mouth on one piece of paper. The fish's open mouth should equal the diameter of the lid. Have each child put the second piece of paper underneath the first and cut out the fish, creating two fish shapes. Have the children decorate the fish shapes with markers or crayons. Then have each child glue the edges of the two fish shapes together but leave the mouth open.

While the fish are drying, give each child a pair of scissors. Have the children poke a hole in the center of their lids and cut out the inside of the plastic, leaving only a quarter- to half-inch rim. (If you have younger children, do this step yourself before class.) Then let each child place the rim inside his or her fish's mouth, fold back the paper over the plastic rim, glue the paper down, and color the edges.

Cut string or yarn to make pieces that are twelve inches long. Use a hole punch to make two holes through each fish's head. Loop the string through both holes, and tie the ends together. Then attach another length of string to the middle of the first one.

Let the children take their windsocks home and hang them from the ceiling or a curtain rod to remind them that they can be fishers of men for Jesus.

MARK
2:1-12

THEME:
We can lead others to Jesus.

SUMMARY:
In this QUIET REFLECTION activity, children think of ways to bring others to Jesus.

PREPARATION: You'll need a Bible, index cards, pencils, tape, chalk, and chalkboard.

Have volunteers take turns reading Mark 2:1-12. Then ask:

■ **Why did the paralyzed man's friends take him to see Jesus?**

■ **Why do you think they wanted their friend to see Jesus?**

■ **Do you know anyone who needs to know Jesus?**

Hand out index cards and pencils. Say: **Think of the people you would like to introduce to Jesus. Draw pictures of those people, one picture per card.**

After the children have finished drawing, say: **The people in the Bible story loved their friend so much that they did something out of the ordinary so their friend could meet Jesus. They actually tore a hole in the roof to lower their friend into the room where Jesus was. Let's think of different ways we can introduce our friends and family members to Jesus. It's OK if our ideas are out of the ordinary. Remember, the goal is to help people meet Jesus.**

Write the word "Jesus" on a chalkboard or piece of newsprint taped to a wall. As a child mentions an idea, have him or her tape one of the drawings under the word "Jesus." Encourage the children to be creative in thinking of ways for their friends to meet Jesus. An out-of-the-ordinary idea might be to plant a garden that spells out "Jesus loves you" and then to invite a friend over to see the garden.

After the children have taped all of their drawings under the word "Jesus," say: **As Christians, one of our biggest jobs is to introduce others to Jesus. There are lots of ways to do that. The people in the Bible story wanted their friend to meet Jesus so much that they did the unthinkable—they lowered him through the roof. We can be just as creative in helping our friends meet Jesus.**

MARK
4:2-8, 13-20

THEME:
It's important to hear God's Word and learn from it.

SUMMARY:
In this CREATIVE STORYTELLING activity, the children act out the parable of the sower.

PREPARATION: You'll need a Bible.

As you read the following story, have the children join you in doing the italicized motions. Say: **Listen to this story that Jesus told about a farmer.**

One day, a farmer decided to plant some seeds. *(Pretend to plant seeds from a shoulder bag.)* **Some seeds fell by the road.** *(Put your hands over your eyebrows as if you're looking down a long road.)* **But birds came and ate up the seeds.** *(Flap your arms like a bird and pretend to swoop down for seeds.)*

The farmer continued to plant his seeds. *(Pretend to plant.)* **Some of the seeds landed in rocky soil.** *(Rub your neck and say "ouch!")* **Even though the plants grew, they died because their roots didn't grow deeply.** *(Slowly curl into a ball, pretending to wilt and shrivel.)*

The farmer planted some more seeds. *(Pretend to plant.)* **Some of the seeds landed among thorny weeds.** *(Crouch down with tucked knees and elbows and say, "Hey, move over!")* **But the weeds grew and crowded out the good plants.** *(Pretend to be thorny weeds, growing tall and over-powering the good seeds.)*

Still the farmer planted. *(Pretend to plant.)* **Some other seeds fell on rich, good ground.** *(Stretch your arms and say "aah!")* **The seeds began to grow.** *(Crouch down and then begin to rise slowly.)* **The plants got taller and taller.** *(Continue rising.)* **And soon the plants produced an abundant crop.** *(Stretch your arms up high and wave them in the wind.)*

Have the children give themselves a big round of applause, then gather everyone together. Open your Bible to Mark 4:13-20, and show children the passage. Say: **Jesus says that the farmer in this story is like a person who plants God's message in people. Let's think about our story again.**

Show me the seeds planted by the road. *(Put your hand over your eyebrows.)* **Jesus says those seeds are like people who hear the word of God, but Satan comes quickly and takes away the teaching that was planted in them.**

Show me the seeds planted on rocky soil. *(Rub your neck and say "ouch!")* **Those seeds are like people who are happy when they hear about God, but they don't let the teaching go deep into their lives. When troubles come, they give up on God.**

Show me the seeds planted among thorny weeds. *(Crouch down with tucked knees and elbows and say, "Hey, move over!")* **Those seeds are like people who are so worried about life that they can't accept the teaching of God. God's Word never grows in their lives because it's crowded out by temptation and sin.**

Show me the seeds planted in good soil. *(Stretch your arms and say "aah!")* **Those seeds are like people who hear the word of God and accept it. Those people grow and produce more good fruit.** Ask:

■ **What does the Bible mean by "good fruit"?**

■ **What can you do to produce good fruit in your life?**

Close in prayer, asking God to make your hearts like the good soil so his Word can grow and produce fruit.

MARK
4:21-23

THEME:
Jesus wants us to share our faith.

SUMMARY:
In this OBJECT LESSON, children discover what happens when a light is hidden under a bowl and learn about sharing their faith.

PREPARATION: You'll need a Bible and candles. (Votive candles in glass holders are sturdy and safe. Birthday candles inserted into mounds of modeling clay are also safe to use.) You'll also need matches and glass jars that fit over the candles.

If your children are younger than eight, do this activity for your class as children watch. Older children can do the activity safely in a quiet and controlled atmosphere.

Have the children form groups of three or four. Give each group a candle and a glass jar. Go around the room and light each group's candle. Have the children sit on their hands so that none of the candles are upset. After all of the candles are lit, have one child in each group put the glass jar over the candle. Have the children watch as the candle burns all of the oxygen inside the jar until the candle goes out. It shouldn't take more than a minute or so for the candles to burn out.

Have a volunteer read Mark 4:21-23 from the Bible. Ask:

■ **What happens when a light is hidden?**

■ **What is the light this passage talks about?**

■ **What happens when we hide the light of our faith?**

■ **How can we make sure that our lights shine?**

Say: **Our belief in God makes us different from much of the world. When others see our light, they see what it's like to follow God. If we hide that light, some people may not ever see what it's like to be a follower of God. And what's more, if we hide our light, it may go out. We may lose our desire to follow God.**

To close, pray: **God, help us to shine our light for all the world to see. Thank you for being such a wonderful God. In Jesus' name, amen.**

MARK
4:30-32

THEME:
We're part of God's kingdom.

SUMMARY:
In this AFFIRMATION ACTIVITY, children learn that those who follow God become part of God's kingdom.

PREPARATION: You'll need a Bible, sticks and twigs, a marker, thick tempera paint in several colors, paintbrushes, newspaper, butcher paper or newsprint, construction paper, and tape.

Before class, tape butcher paper or newsprint to a wall. Draw or paint a simple tree trunk on the butcher paper. Include a few sketched-in branches. The children will attach sticks and twigs to the tree trunk to create the branches, so keep the trunk in proportion to the size and number of sticks you'll be using. Also, tear small leaf shapes from colored construction paper. You'll need several leaves for each child.

Give each child a stick or a twig and some newspaper. The sticks should be about a foot long and no more than one-fourth inch in diameter. Using the newspaper to catch drips, have the children paint the sticks in designs that represent their likes or their talents. For example, one child may paint his stick green and yellow because those are the colors of his soccer team. Set the sticks aside to dry.

Say: **In church we often talk about the kingdom of God. Listen to what Jesus says.** Read Mark 4:30-32 aloud.

Say: **Christians are part of God's kingdom. We need to follow God and do what he asks of us. Let's pretend that the tree trunk on the wall represents God and the branches represent members of his kingdom. We'll attach our painted sticks to the tree trunk to show that each of us can be a part of God's kingdom.**

Help the children tape their sticks to the tree trunk to look like tree branches.

When the sticks are all attached, say: **I see each of you following God.** Affirm each child with the following sentence: (Child's name), **I see you following God when you...** Complete the sentence with words such as "share with others" or "treat guests with kindness." Then give that child a leaf and a piece of tape, and have the child tape the leaf to his or her branch.

Continue until every child has been affirmed. Encourage older children to affirm each other in this activity.

MARK 4:35-41

THEME:
Jesus is more powerful than anyone or anything.

SUMMARY:
In this LEARNING GAME, the children act out Jesus' miracle of calming the storm.

PREPARATION: You'll need Bibles.

Have children form pairs and number off within their pairs from one to two. Have all the ones read Mark 4:35-38 and all the twos read Mark 4:39-41.

Afterward, say: **What an exciting story! Jesus' followers must have been scared in that storm.** Ask:

■ **Have you ever been in a scary storm?**

■ **What are some other times you've been afraid?**

After kids share some of their scary experiences, say: **We're all afraid sometimes, but it's great to know that Jesus is always taking care of us. Let's play a game called Stormy Seas to remind us of our Bible story.**

Have all the ones line up against one wall of the room. The ones will be the Followers in the boat. The twos will scatter around the room. They'll be the stormy Waves.

When you give a signal, the Followers will try to "row" across the room to the opposite wall and back by making rowing motions with their arms. The Waves will try to tag the Followers as they row. Encourage the Waves to move their arms up and down and make wind and thunder noises.

A Wave can't tag a Follower if the Follower first says, "Be still!" If a Wave does tag a Follower, the Follower becomes a Wave and joins in the tagging.

After a few minutes of play, call time; then have the children switch roles. After a few more minutes, call time again. Then say: **Jesus can calm all of the stormy times in our lives. Let's do the "wave" and give God a group cheer to thank him for using his power to take care of us.** Have kids form a circle, then start a wave around the circle as you cheer, "Yeah, God!"

MARK
5:21-24, 35-43

THEME:
We can trust in Jesus' power.

SUMMARY:
In this MUSIC IDEA, children celebrate Jesus' power in raising Jairus' daughter from the dead.

PREPARATION: You'll need Bibles.

Have children form pairs and number off from one to two within their pairs. Have the ones read Mark 5:21-24 and the twos read Mark 5:35-43. Then gather everyone in a circle.

Lead the children in singing the following song to the tune of the chorus of "Our God Is an Awesome God." After the first verse, have the children share what they've seen Jesus do in their lives and in the lives of their friends and families. For example, a child might say that he was protected in a traffic accident. Another child might say that Jesus healed her from an illness.

After the second verse, have the children mention ways Jesus will care for them in the future. For example, a child might say that Jesus will care for her when she is sick, poor, hungry, or sad.

Verse 1
Believe in Jesus' power.
He can do anything.
He brings the dead to life.
Believe in Jesus' power.

Verse 2
**Don't be afraid, my friend.
The Lord will care for you.
Believe in Jesus' love.
Believe in Jesus' power.**

MARK
6:34-44

THEME:
Jesus can do miracles.

SUMMARY:
In this OBJECT LESSON, children learn how a little can go a long way and how Jesus fed five thousand men with just two fish and five loaves of bread.

PREPARATION: You'll need a Bible, unpopped popcorn, an electric popcorn popper, a see-through measuring cup, napkins, and a large bowl.

Before this activity, prepare the popcorn popper for use.

Say: **Today we're going to see how a little can go a long way.**

Gather kids in a circle around a work table. Open the container of unpopped popcorn, and give each child a small handful of kernels. Say: **This amount of popcorn ought to keep the hunger away, don't you think?** Kids will probably answer that they'd like more.

Say: **It doesn't look like much—that's true. Maybe if we put all of our kernels together, it'll be enough.**

Go around the circle, asking each child to put his or her kernels into the see-through measuring cup. Note where the popcorn comes to in the measuring cup. Then hold up the cup and say: **Well, it still doesn't look like much, but let's give it a try.**

Pour the popcorn from the measuring cup into the popper. Have children wash their hands, then choose a few volunteers to distribute napkins. As kids are preparing for their snack, pour enough popcorn kernels into the measuring cup to reach the same level they did before.

When the kernels finish popping, pour the popcorn into a bowl. Hold up the bowl of popcorn and the measuring cup of kernels and say: **Wow! Look at the difference. A little bit of popcorn really did go a long way! You know, this reminds me of a story from the Bible. Let me read it to you.**

Pass around the bowl of popcorn, and read Mark 6:34-44 aloud as kids enjoy their snack. Ask:

■ **Did you think that little bit of popcorn would be enough to feed all of us? Why or why not?**

■ **What do you think Jesus' followers thought when they saw that they only had two fish and five loaves of bread to feed all those people?**

■ **How do you think you would have felt if you had been one of the five thousand fed that day?**

Say: **Jesus cared about the people, so he used God's help to make sure they had enough to eat. Jesus cares about us, too, and will always take care of us. Isn't that great to know? Let's give God a great big cheer!**

To close, have kids shout together, "Hooray for God!"

MARK 6:45-51

THEME:
Even nature obeys Jesus.

SUMMARY:
In this CREATIVE STORYTELLING activity, the children act out the story of Jesus walking on the water.

PREPARATION: You'll need a Bible and paper.

If some children in your group are able to read, you may want to photocopy this story and distribute copies to your readers so they can follow along and help others with the italicized motions in the parentheses.

You'll need one child to be Jesus and two to be Followers. Everyone else will be the Waves.

Have the Waves sit in a wide circle, and give each one a sheet of paper. Have the two Followers sit together inside the circle and pretend to row a boat. Have the child playing Jesus stand outside the circle. Have the children join you in doing the italicized motions during the story.

Say: **Let's pretend we're there the night Jesus will walk on water.**

We're rowing across the lake at night toward Bethsaida. *(Followers pretend to row.)* **It sure is dark tonight. We can't even see the hills where Jesus stayed to pray.** *(Followers shield eyes as if looking toward shore and then continue to row.)* **At least the waves are gentle and the breeze is mild.** *(Waves slowly fan their sheets of paper up and down and make gentle whooshing sounds. Followers slowly row.)*

What's that noise? The wind seems to be picking up. *(Waves fan papers faster and make louder whooshing noises. Followers row harder.)* **Oh, no! It looks like a storm! It's getting harder and harder to row against the wind.** *(Followers row harder as Waves fan faster and make storm noises.)*

This is terrible! What if we drown? I'm so scared! *(Followers struggle with pretend oars as Waves quickly fan papers.)* **I wonder if Jesus knows what's happening to us?** *(The child playing Jesus puts hand over eyebrows and looks toward the boat, then steps into the "lake" and walks toward the Followers.)*

What's that? What is it? I can barely see through the rain and waves. It...it...looks like... it can't be! Is it a ghost? Oh, no! Oh, help! *(Followers crouch in fear as Waves continue storming.)*

Wait! I know that voice! Could it really be? *(The child playing Jesus says, "Have courage! It is I. Do not be afraid." Followers peer into the storm. Waves continue fanning the papers.)*

It is! It's Jesus! *(Waves stop fanning the papers. The child playing Jesus steps into the boat. The Followers hold their arms up toward him.)*

We're safe! Jesus made the storm stop! *(Followers clap and cheer. Waves slowly fan their papers.)* Thank you, Jesus, for saving our lives! You can do anything!

MARK
8:34-38

THEME:
It's not always easy to follow Jesus.

SUMMARY:
In this active DEVOTION, the children learn what it means to count the cost of discipleship.

PREPARATION: You'll need a Bible, tape, butcher paper or newsprint, a marker, paper, and pencils.

EXPERIENCE

Have the children form pairs, encouraging older children to pair up with younger children. Give each pair a pencil and a sheet of paper.

Say: **Pretend that you want to buy a new bicycle. Your parents think it's a good idea, and they're willing to give you half of the money. The bike you want costs ninety dollars. Since your parents will pay half, you** need to come up with forty-five dollars.

Unfortunately, you've spent all of your allowance, and you don't have any money saved. You need to earn the entire forty-five dollars. With your partner, come up with a plan to earn the money.

Give the children several minutes to develop plans. Then ask the following questions, and have pairs share their responses with the rest of the class.

■ **How did you decide to come up with the money?**

■ **What will you have to give up to make your plan work?**

■ **Do you think buying a new bicycle would be worth the extra work and time it would take to earn the money?**

■ **How do you decide whether or not something is worth doing?**

Say: **People set all kinds of goals for themselves. Often, they have to give up things that won't help them reach those goals. If your goal is to save money for a bicycle, you may have to give up some things to reach your goal.** Ask:

■ **What are some goals people set for themselves?**

■ **What might they have to give up to reach their goals?**

■ **Why are people willing to give up things to reach their goals?**

RESPONSE

Say: **Jesus talked about giving up less important things to reach a greater goal. Let's read about it.** Have a volunteer read

Mark 8:34-38. Ask:
■ **What goal is Jesus talking about?**
Say: **Let's consider the costs and rewards of following God, just as we considered buying a bike.**
Tape a piece of butcher paper or newsprint to the wall. With a marker, divide the paper into two columns. Write "Rewards" at the top of one column and "Costs" at the top of the other. Write kids' responses to the following questions in the appropriate columns. Encourage the children to refer to the Bible passage. Ask:
■ **What do you have to give up to follow God? What will following God "cost" you?**
■ **What are the rewards of following God?**
■ **Is following God worth it? Explain.**

CLOSING
Give each child another piece of paper. Hand out additional pencils. Say: **On your paper, write or draw the costs of following God that are hardest for you. Then write or draw the reward that means the most to you.**
After children have finished writing and drawing, invite kids to spend a few moments in silent prayer, thanking God for making the rewards of following him worth the costs.

MARK
10:13-16

THEME:
Jesus loves all children.

SUMMARY:
In this OBJECT LESSON, children experiment with magnets and learn that Jesus loves them and wants to draw them close to him.

PREPARATION: You'll need a Bible, at least two magnets, large paper clips, scissors, crayons, tape, and paper. You'll also need a sheet of thin cardboard and a figure to represent Jesus. (You could tape a flannel-board figure of Jesus to a cardboard cutout or simply make your own simple cutout before class.)

Have the children form pairs. Supply several crayons for each pair, and give each child a sheet of paper. Have children draw and decorate pictures of themselves. Make sure they write their names on the front of the pictures. Then have them cut out their pictures. (Have older children help younger children with cutting.) Show children how to make a triple accordion-fold along the bottom of the picture, then paper clip the folds together at each end. The picture should then stand upright.
Place the figure of Jesus on one end of the cardboard. Let the children stand their pictures on the other end of the cardboard. Allow children to take turns holding the

magnets on the underside of the cardboard. They can use the magnets to make the pictures of themselves move closer to Jesus.

For extra fun, younger children will enjoy standing on one side of the room and pretending that Jesus' love is drawing them like a magnet to the other side.

After all the children have had a chance to move their pictures with the magnets, gather the children in a circle. Then read aloud Mark 10:13-16. Ask:

■ **Why did the parents want their children to be with Jesus?**

■ **How did Jesus react to the children?**

■ **Why does Jesus love children?**

■ **How does Jesus feel about you?**

Put two magnets together, and show the children how the magnets are drawn to each other. Pass the magnets around so kids can feel how they pull toward each other. Say: **Jesus' love is like a magnet. It draws us to him. Let's thank**

God right now for his love which draws us near to him. Close by letting children take turns using a magnet to pull their pictures closer to the figure of Jesus as they say, "Thank you, Jesus, for drawing me closer to you."

MARK
10:17-31

THEME:
It's not always easy to find your way to heaven.

SUMMARY:
In this LEARNING GAME, children discover how difficult it is for a camel to go through the eye of a needle.

PREPARATION: You'll need a Bible and four adult-sized folding chairs.

Line up the four adult-sized folding chairs. They should be touching each other, side by side, with the seats all facing the same direction. This will create a tunnel, which represents the eye of the needle, between the legs of the chairs.

Have children take turns reading the verses in Mark 10:17-31 from the Bible. Ask:

■ **Why do you think it's hard for rich people to get into heaven?**

■ **Is it wrong to have money? Why or why not?**

■ **Why do you think Jesus**

used the image of a camel going through the eye of a needle to illustrate his point?

■ **What other kinds of things could make it hard for us to reach heaven?**

Say: **Let's play a game to remind us of this Bible passage. These chairs will be the eye of the needle, and all of you will be Camels. It will be your job to crawl through the eye of the needle.**

Have the children line up and take turns crawling through the eye of the needle. They'll probably end up on their bellies, wiggling through the chairs. Make sure the second child doesn't start through the tunnel until the first child is all the way through. If you have more than eight children, set up two tunnels for them to crawl through.

If the children in your class are little ones, tie small pillows or folded towels to their backs with socks or nylon hose. This will make it more challenging to crawl through, and they'll look more like camels.

For extra fun, turn this game into a relay race. Make two tunnels, and have children form two teams. The winning team is the first one whose members have all crawled through the eye of the needle.

MARK
12:28-34

THEME:
We can love God and our neighbors.

SUMMARY:
In this SERVICE PROJECT, the children learn how to love God and their neighbor as they love themselves.

PREPARATION: You'll need a Bible, construction paper, tape, scissors, paper, and pens.

Make a large construction paper cross to hang on one wall of your classroom. Hang the cross so that the crossbeam is still within reach of the children.

Ask a volunteer to read Mark 12:28-34. Ask:

■ **How can we love God with all our heart, all our soul, all our mind, and all our strength?**

■ **How can we love our neighbor as we love ourselves?**

Say: **Let's think of specific actions we can do to fulfill both parts of this commandment.**

Have the children brainstorm about how to fulfill this commandment. Write each of their ideas at the top of a separate piece of white paper. Children could name such ways to love God as praying for five minutes before going to bed, singing a praise song while taking a shower, or reading one chapter from the Bible every day. They could name such ways to love their neighbors as making cookies for new neighbors, walking on the sidewalk instead of trampling through a neighbor's yard, or taking flowers to a sick neighbor.

Attach the sheets of paper that deal with loving God to the vertical beam of the cross. Attach the sheets that talk about loving neighbors on the horizontal beam of the cross. Give the children pens, and have them write their names on the actions they'd like to try during the coming week.

Leave the cross up for several weeks. When children finish a task, they can initial and date the actions beside their names. Remind them frequently to sign up for more activities and to think of more service actions they can add to the cross. Be sure to ask the children how their neighbors and friends are responding to their actions and how their relationship with God is developing.

MARK
13:32-37

THEME:
We must be ready to follow Jesus all the time.

SUMMARY:
In this active DEVOTION, children learn the importance of being ready for Jesus.

PREPARATION: You'll need a Bible and masking tape or string.

EXPERIENCE

Say: **We're going to run a race. But in this race, we're not going to pay attention to the *end* of the race but rather to the *beginning* of the race.**

Have the children line up for a race outside or in a large room. If you're inside, use masking tape to mark a starting line and a finish line. If you're outside, use string.

Position each child in a different stance to begin the race. For example, have one child squat down with one knee and both hands on the ground as if using a starting block. Have another child simply stand at the starting line. Have another child sit, one child stand with legs crossed, one child face backward, and another child start from ten feet back. Come up with a different starting stance for each child.

Before you begin the race, ask:

■ **From the way you're all positioned, who do you predict is most likely to win the race?**

Start the race. After everyone has reached the finish line, gather the children together and ask:

■ **Did the race go as you expected?**

■ **Was this a fair race? Why or why not?**

■ **What happened in the race that held some people back?**

■ **What gave some people an advantage?**

■ **What happened to the people who were ready for the race?**

■ **What happened to the people who were not ready?**

RESPONSE

Say: **In this race, the way I positioned you determined how** ready you were to run. There's a passage in the Bible that talks about readiness. Let's read it. Have children take turns reading Mark 13:32-37. Ask:

■ **What does this passage say we should be ready for?**

■ **What are some people doing instead of getting ready for Jesus?**

■ **How can we get ready for Jesus?**

CLOSING

Say: **To demonstrate how important it is to be ready for Jesus, let's run the race again. Determine the starting position that you think will make you the most ready for the race.**

When the children are ready for the race, say: **All of you are ready for the race. You're in position, you're focused, and you're paying attention. As we look for Jesus' return, we need to be focused on Jesus, too.**

When I say, "Run to Jesus," run toward the finish line and pretend that you're running toward Jesus when he returns. It won't matter who gets there first. It only matters that you're ready for Jesus' return. We won't name a winner in this race, but we'll give praise when we all reach the finish line.

Say, "Run to Jesus" to start the race. After the race, have the children huddle together and cheer, "We'll be ready! We'll be ready! Yeah, Jesus!"

MARK 14:22-26

THEME:

We can remember Jesus with love.

SUMMARY:

In this CRAFT activity, the children create a box to hold reminders of Jesus.

PREPARATION: You'll need a Bible, shoe boxes or other small boxes, tissue paper, old greeting cards, old wrapping paper, scissors, and markers. You'll also need white glue, water, shallow bowls, and paintbrushes. Dilute the white glue by adding an equal ratio of water to the glue.

Give each child a shoe box and a paintbrush. Set out several colors of tissue paper and old greeting cards and wrapping paper.

Explain to the children that they are to cover their boxes with tissue paper by painting white glue on a section of the box, tearing off a piece of tissue paper, pressing it onto the box, and painting over the paper with the white glue. Explain to the children that the craft works best if they cover the edges of the boxes' openings first and then turn their boxes so the wet sides of the boxes aren't on the table top. Have the children work until their boxes are completely covered.

Then have children cut symbols from greeting cards and wrapping paper that remind them of Jesus. They can cut existing shapes from the cards and paper or think of their own shapes to cut out. They may want to cut out heart shapes to remind them of Jesus' love, crosses to remind them of Jesus' death, or stars to remind them of Jesus' birth.

Have children attach the pictures they've cut out to their boxes in the same way they attached the tissue paper.

As the children work, say: **As you work, listen while I read a passage from the Bible about remembering Jesus.** Read Mark 14:22-26. Then ask:

■ **What was the bread to remind the disciples of?**

■ **What was the wine to remind the disciples of?**

■ **Why is it important to remember Jesus?**

■ **What might have happened if the disciples had forgotten about Jesus?**

■ **What would you like to remember about Jesus?**

Say: **After these boxes have dried, you may put things inside that remind you of Jesus.** Ask:

■ **What could you put inside to help you remember Jesus?**

Children's answers may include Bibles, a piece of rough wood, or a twig from a thorn branch.

Say: **It's important to remember Jesus. We need to remember that he loves us so much that he was willing to die on the cross for our sins. And what a joy it is to remember that he rose again so that if we believe in him, we can have eternal life with him. Keep these boxes in your rooms as a way of remembering Jesus' love and sacrifice.**

MARK 14:66-72

THEME:

It's important to honor our commitment to God.

SUMMARY:

Use this QUIET REFLECTION to help children consider the depth of their commitment to God.

PREPARATION: You'll need a Bible, paper, pencils, and scissors.

Have the children scatter around the room and sit down where they won't distract each other. Give each child a pencil and a sheet of paper. Have volunteers take turns reading Mark 14:66-72. Ask :

■ **Why didn't Peter follow through on his promise to never deny Christ?**

■ **How do you think Peter felt when he was asked if he knew Christ?**

Say: **Sometimes we all fall short of our good intentions.** Ask:

■ **Have you ever had good intentions that you didn't follow through with?**

■ **How did you feel about not following through?**

■ **Peter denied Jesus by saying he didn't know him. How do people deny Jesus today?**

Say: **Write the numbers one through ten on your sheet of paper. Consider how deep your commitment to Jesus is, and circle the number you feel indicates your level of commitment.**

The number ten indicates a very high commitment, and a one indicates a low commitment. No one else will see your paper.

Next, write down one area in your life in which you have a hard time keeping your commitment to follow God. After you're finished writing, fold your paper twice with the writing inside.

Have the children bring their papers and sit in a circle with you.

Say: **Peter's story is something we can all relate to. We all have grand intentions of how we're going to follow God. Following through can be a whole different story, though. But there's good news.**

Jesus knew that Peter would make this mistake. And Jesus loved Peter in spite of his failings. Jesus forgave Peter and gave him a second chance. Peter repented of his sin and went on to become one of the most persuasive preachers and leaders in the early church.

Give each child a pair of scissors. Have children cut their papers into tiny pieces and throw the pieces away in a trash can or recycling bin.

End with this prayer: **God, thank you for knowing us inside and out. You know when we will fail and when we will succeed. Thank you for loving us all the time. Help us to deepen our commitment to you every day. Amen.**

MARK
15:33-39

THEME:
Jesus died for us.

SUMMARY:
In this MUSIC IDEA, the children express sorrow for Jesus' death and joy for his resurrection.

PREPARATION: You'll need a Bible and a variety of rhythm instruments such as tambourines, rhythm sticks, and sand blocks. (If such instruments are unavailable, use pots and pans, sticks, sandpaper glued to wood blocks, and jingle bells.) You'll also need paper and a pencil.

Say: **We make music to express the way we feel. Sometimes our music is happy. But when we're sad, we make music that sounds sad, too.**

Read the story of Jesus' death from Mark 15:33-39. Ask:

■ **Why did Jesus die?**

■ **How do you think Jesus' disciples felt when he died?**

■ **How does Jesus' death make you feel?**

Write the children's responses on a sheet of paper. Say: **Let's make sad music with these rhythm instruments to remind us how Jesus' disciples must have felt that day. When I hold my hand with the palm up and open, that's your signal to make music. When I close my hand into a fist, that's your signal to stop making music.**

Listen to these words and then make music to match the words. Read some of the responses to the questions above. Then hold your hand open with the palm facing up. After thirty seconds, close your hand into a fist. Then read more of the responses, and signal the children to make music again.

Stop the music again, and say: **It was a sad day when Jesus died, but there's much more to the story.** Ask:

■ **What happened on the third day after Jesus died?**

Say: **That's right! Jesus rose and lives with God in heaven.** Ask:

■ **How does it make you feel to know that Jesus is alive today?**

Say: **Now let's make happy music with our instruments to celebrate Jesus' resurrection.** Hold your palm open to have the children make happy music for about a minute.

Say: **That was wonderful music! I'm so happy that Jesus is alive today. Let's thank God for that right now.** Pray: **Jesus, thank you for dying for us. We're happy to know that you are alive today. We praise you, Jesus. Amen.**

MARK
16:1-7

THEME:
Jesus triumphed over death.

SUMMARY:
From this TRIPS 'N' TRAVELS activity, children learn that dying is a hopeful experience for those who love God.

PREPARATION: Before this activity, make arrangements to visit a cemetery with your class. Have each child bring a written permission slip from a parent or guardian to participate. You'll need to bring a Bible, tracing paper, and charcoals or crayons. You'll also need snacks and beverages to serve after your outing.

TEACHER TIP
Be sensitive to any children in your class who may have recently experienced the loss of a loved one. You may want to save this activity for a more appropriate time.

Take your children on a trip to visit a local cemetery. If it is permitted, take tracing paper and charcoals or crayons to make rubbings of the headstones. Have the children look at the headstones and notice the names of the people who are buried there. Have them notice how old the people were when they died. Note families that are buried together. In particular, have children look for headstones with religious epitaphs. Also notice the care that is taken to keep the cemetery beautiful.

If the children have made rubbings, have them show the rubbings to each other. Then put the rubbings aside, and gather the children in a circle. Ask:

■ **Do you find cemeteries peaceful and restful or creepy and scary? Explain.**

■ **Why are we sad when people die?**

Have the children take turns reading Mark 16:1-7. Ask:

■ **What does Jesus' resurrection mean to you?**

■ **How does Jesus' resurrection change the way we think of cemeteries?**

Say: **Cemeteries can make ev-eryone feel kind of creepy sometimes because we know that all people will die someday—even us. But for people who love God, dying doesn't have to be scary. Those who love God can be hopeful because we know that we'll live with Jesus in heaven. Jesus' resurrection makes that a sure thing! Let's go back to our classroom and celebrate that great news!**

After you return to your classroom, serve snacks and beverages to celebrate the good news of Jesus' resurrection. Before you enjoy the treats, say a prayer thanking God for the awesome gift of eternal life through faith in Jesus.

LUKE

"Today your Savior was born in the town of David. He is Christ, the Lord."

Luke 2:11

LUKE 1:46-55

THEME:
God wants us to praise him.

SUMMARY:
Use this creative PRAYER to encourage children to think of reasons to praise God.

PREPARATION: You'll need a Bible and a noisemaker.

Have a volunteer read Luke 1:46-55 to the rest of the class. Then say: **In this passage, Mary praised God for his goodness, and we can praise God too. Let's say an "up, down, all around" praise prayer!**

Have children sit cross-legged in a circle. Tell them to tap out a rhythm as they say, "Up, down, all around!" Show children how to tap twice on their knees, then clap twice in time to the words. When everyone understands the rhythm, add a twist. As everyone continues tapping and clapping, have children say the phrase in sequence, each child saying one word as the phrase goes around the circle.

Periodically sound the noisemaker. Whoever is speaking when you sound the noisemaker will tell one reason to praise God. For example, if you sound the noisemaker on the word "up," the child whose turn it is could stop and say, "I praise God for giving us bright sunshine" or "I praise God for the clouds that bring rain."

For extra fun, vary the tempo of

the praise prayer. Continue until everyone in the circle has had a chance to praise God. Then lead the class in an enthusiastic "hip, hip, hooray" cheer for God!

LUKE
1:76-80

THEME:
We can prepare for Jesus.

SUMMARY:
Use this MUSIC IDEA to help kids experience the excitement of the message brought by John the Baptist.

PREPARATION: You'll need a Bible and a variety of simple percussion instruments such as spoons, sticks, and empty coffee cans with lids. If you have time, let children make their own instruments during this activity. Provide materials such as paper cups, dry beans, plastic wrap, tape, empty plastic bottles, and empty soft drink cans.

Before this activity, make sure the cans and bottles are clean and have no sharp edges.

Set out the simple instruments. If you're making instruments, set out bottles, cans, cups, beans, plastic wrap, and tape.

Say: **Before Jesus was born, God sent a man called John the Baptist to help people get ready for Jesus.** Ask a volunteer to read Luke 1:76-80 aloud.

Then say: **Jesus was coming, and John the Baptist wanted everyone to be ready! We can get ready for Jesus too. Today we're going to follow in John's footsteps and learn a way to share the good news that Jesus will come again.**

Teach children this rhythmic message: Pre-pare-the-way-of-the-Lord! Hal-le-LU-ia!

Invite each child to choose an instrument. If you're making instruments, help children partially fill the cups, bottles, or cans with dry beans and then seal the tops with plastic wrap and tape.

After children have learned the rhythm, practice saying the message while playing the instruments, increasing and decreasing the tempo and volume. Encourage children to come up with the most intricate rhythm patterns they can.

Say: **When I say, "Jesus is coming," switch instruments with someone else!**

Lead a parade during which children repeat the message and play instruments, varying the volume and speed. Have them visit other Sunday school classes, or, if possible, have children deliver the message as a call to worship at the beginning of the church service. Invite adults to join the parade. At a prearranged signal, finish together with a rousing cheer!

LUKE
2:1-7

THEME:
Jesus is the greatest gift of all.

SUMMARY:
This PARTY helps kids focus on what a gift God has given us in Jesus.

PREPARATION: You'll need a Bible; small, individually wrapped treats that are marked for each child in your class; and party supplies as described below for the activities you choose.

Before class, hide the wrapped treats in various places around the room.

As children arrive, tell them that you're going to have a birthday party for Jesus! Begin by having a volunteer read Luke 2:1-7. Then say: **Mary and Joseph had to travel a long way before Jesus was born. We have to travel a bit, too, before we can enjoy our party.**

Explain that there's a gift for each child hidden somewhere in the room. Let children travel about the room, hunting for their gifts. Be sure to remind children that no one should disturb a gift intended for someone else and that no one should say where he or she has seen a gift with another child's name on it.

When all of the children have located their gifts, have them place the gifts on a table. Before opening the gifts, enjoy some of the following "gifty" games.

Have a Christmas-present relay. Place tape and two gift-wrapped and ribbon-tied boxes on a table at one end of the room. Form two teams, and have them line up at the opposite end of the room. When you say "go," a child from each team will hurry to the table, untie and unwrap the gift box, then rewrap and retie the box. Then each child will tag the next person in line.

Or play Gift Giveaway. Give each child ten wrapped Christmas candies. Whenever a player can get another child to answer a question with "yes" or "no," the player hands the answering child a candy. The idea is to get rid of all ten candies by giving them away to others.

If you want to include a Christmas piñata at your party, let children create the piñata by decorating a paper sack and by filling the sack with wrapped candies.

For another fun holiday game, let children play Shining Stars. Cut large stars from yellow construction paper, and tape them at various heights and places along the walls of the room. Make one star less than you have children in your group. Have children march in a circle in the center of the room as you play a cassette of Christmas music. When you stop the music, children must scurry to touch a shining star. Any players without a star should link arms with a child touching a star. Remove a star before starting the music again, and continue playing this Christmasy version of Musical Chairs.

After the games, let children unwrap their gifts. As they enjoy the treats, talk about what a wonderful gift God gave us when he sent his Son, Jesus, into the world.

LUKE
2:8-18

THEME:
We can share the news about Jesus.

SUMMARY:
From this OBJECT LESSON, children learn how the shepherds may have felt when the angels appeared in the night sky, and children send a sparkling message about Jesus' birth.

PREPARATION: You'll need a Bible, dark-colored construction paper, small paintbrushes, a teaspoon, cups, water, salt, and access to an oven.

Say: **Today we're going to send a message in an amazing way.**

Give each child a sheet of dark-colored construction paper, a paintbrush, and a cup of water containing three teaspoons of salt. Have children create a Christmas scene telling the news of Jesus' birth. Tell children to dip and stir with the brush before writing each letter or drawing each image.

As children work, preheat the oven to 150 degrees. Bake the finished scenes for five minutes or until the papers dry. The images will appear as sparkling crystals on the dark paper.

After the pictures are finished, set them aside and ask a volunteer to read aloud Luke 2:8-18. Ask:

■ **What did you think when I gave you saltwater instead of paint?**

■ **Were you surprised at how your amazing messages turned out? Explain.**

■ **How do you think the shepherds felt when they heard the angels' message?**

■ **If you had been with the shepherds that night, how would you have reacted?**

Say: The angels brought wonderful news to the shepherds that night long ago. Although the shepherds must have been surprised at the message, they went to Bethlehem and found baby Jesus, just as the angels had promised. They told everyone what the angels had said, and everyone who heard the news was amazed.

We can share the amazing news of Jesus too. Take home your amazing message, and give it to someone you'd like to tell about Jesus.

Close in prayer, thanking God for sending Jesus to us.

LUKE
2:41-49

THEME:
It's important to worship God.

SUMMARY:
During this QUIET REFLECTION, kids take a quiet tour of the church building to learn more about the parts of God's house and what takes place there.

PREPARATION: You'll need a Bible.

You may want to invite your pastor to participate in the tour of the church by explaining the function of each area and/or the historical reasons behind its inclusion in a modern church.

Have a volunteer read aloud Luke 2:41-49. Say: **Even though Jesus was still a child, he knew it was important to be in God's house, learning about and worshiping God. Let's take a tour to learn more about this house of God. Remember to be quiet so we don't disturb anyone else.**

Lead the group—with the pastor, if possible—on a tour of the church. Include the narthex, the sanctuary, the altar area, the pulpit, and the lectern. Discuss what the pastor and the people do in each area. If the pastor is present, he or she may contribute information about historical uses of the different areas. Allow children to experience standing in the pulpit, behind the altar, in the choir loft, or sitting at the organ.

After you return to your classroom, ask the children to describe their favorite parts of the church. Ask:

■ **What's special about God's house?**

■ **Why do people come together to worship God?**

■ **Why is it important to worship God?**

Close by praying: **Jesus, you loved to be in your Father's house. Help us to want to come to your house. Help us to learn all we can about you and to worship you every day of our lives. Amen.**

LUKE
4:1-13

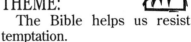

THEME:
The Bible helps us resist temptation.

SUMMARY:
Use this LEARNING GAME to help kids understand that God's Word can help us resist temptation.

PREPARATION: You'll need Bibles, scrap paper, pencils and markers, masking tape, and large pieces of cardboard or poster board.

Have children form pairs. If you have young children who cannot read, pair nonreaders with readers. Within the pairs, have children number off from one to two. Have the ones read aloud Luke 4:1-6 in their pairs; then have the twos read aloud Luke 4:7-13. Say: **Let's play a game to remind us that we can use God's Word to resist temptation.**

Have the ones gather on one side of the room. Give them pencils and scrap paper. Tell them to write or draw temptations they face every day on the pieces of scrap paper. They might write temptations such as cheating in school or fighting with a brother or sister. Have children crumple each temptation into a paper wad.

As the ones are working, have the twos gather on the other side of the room. Give them markers, scrap paper, masking tape, and the large pieces of cardboard. Have them make Bible shields by writing, "The Bible" on one side of the cardboard and by taping a paper wad to the other side of the cardboard to form a handle.

When you say, "go," have the twos try to cross to the other side of the room and back as the ones try to pelt them with the paper-wad temptations. The twos may use their Bible shields as protection. Then have the ones and twos switch roles to play again.

After the game, ask:

∎ **What was it like to have paper wads thrown at you?**

∎ **How were the paper wads like temptations in real life?**

∎ **How did the cardboard shields protect you in our game?**

∎ **How can the Bible protect you from real temptations?**

Hold up your Bible and say: **God's Word is powerful and true! The Bible can teach us, comfort us, and protect us when temptations seem to be all around us. Let's thank God for his amazing Word.** Close with a prayer thanking God for giving us his Word.

LUKE
5:1-11

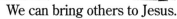

THEME:
We can bring others to Jesus.

SUMMARY:
In this LEARNING GAME, children hear how Jesus told the disciples to be fishers of men and then play a "fishy" variation of Tag.

PREPARATION: You'll need a Bible.

Have children form trios, being sure to mix readers with non-readers. Then have children number off within their groups. Have the ones read Luke 5:1-3, the twos read Luke 5:4-7, and the threes read Luke 5:8-11.

Say: **Today we're going to practice "fishing" for people as Jesus said the disciples would do.**

Have children line up on one side of the room. They'll be the Fish. Choose one child to be the Net. The Net will stand in the center of the room, facing the rest of the class, and call out:

I'm a fisher,
A fisher of men.
Swim for the shore
As I count to ten.

As the Net counts to ten, all the Fish will try to "swim" to the other side of the room without being tagged. Any Fish who is tagged must link arms with the Net and try to catch other Fish.

After all the children have either made it across the room or been tagged, play again. All the children who are part of the Net will recite the rhyme together, count to ten, and try to catch the remaining Fish. Continue the game until all the Fish have been caught. The last Fish to be caught will become the Net to begin the next game.

LUKE
7:36-50

THEME:
Jesus forgives our sins.

SUMMARY:
In this CREATIVE STORYTELLING activity, children pretend to visit Jesus with a sinful woman to learn about his forgiveness.

PREPARATION: You'll need a Bible.

THE FORGIVENESS TRIP

Open your Bible to Luke 7:36-50 to show children the passage. Say:

This Bible story is about a sinful woman who received forgiveness from Jesus. Let's pretend we're listening to the woman. Have the children join you in doing the italicized motions throughout the story.

Have you heard about Jesus? *(Cup your hand around your ear.)* **Well I just heard that a Pharisee who lives nearby asked Jesus to come to his house to eat. I'm going over there right now.** *(Point with an outstretched arm.)* **I'm going to take this beautiful white jar of perfume with me.** *(Pretend to hold out a jar in front of you.)* **Come with me!** *(Wave "come on.")* **We'll see if we can get in to see Jesus. Let's run!** *(Run in place.)* **Oops! I tripped and almost dropped my jar!** *(Pretend to stumble and catch the jar as it falls.)*

Here we are. We'll knock on the door. *(Knock on a pretend door and tap your foot.)* **Maybe they can't hear me. Let's try the door. It's open, but it's heavy!** *(Groan while pretending to open a heavy door.)*

Can you see Jesus? *(Stand on your tiptoes with your hand over your eyebrows as if peering into a crowd.)* **There he is!** *(Point excitedly.)* **Excuse me! Excuse me! I need to get past! Excuse me!** *(Squirm and struggle to get through the crowd.)*

I'm right behind him! I can't believe I'm actually in his presence. *(Put your hands over your mouth in awe.)* **Oh, I've done so many wrong things. I shouldn't even be near Jesus.** *(Kneel and pretend to cry.)* **I'm worse than the lowest servant who washes the feet of the guests.** *(Pretend to wash Jesus' feet as you wipe away tears.)* **I know I'm a terrible sinner. But it's so wonderful just to be near Jesus.**

Where's my jar of perfume? *(Pretend to look around on the floor while still kneeling.)* **Here it is. I'll give it all to Jesus to soothe his feet.** *(Pretend to pour perfume from the jar onto Jesus' feet.)*

I know that Pharisee is looking at me. His eyes look so accusing. *(Look from left to right as you continue to pour perfume.)* **He's probably thinking, "What is that sinful woman doing, kneeling at Jesus' feet?"** *(Put your hands on your hips and frown.)* **But wait. Is Jesus talking about me?** *(Point to yourself.)* **What is he saying?** *(Cup your hand behind your ear.)* **My sins are forgiven?** *(Put your hands out with your palms held up.)* **Mine?** *(Put your hand over your chest.)* **He loves me that much? Oh, Jesus,**

thank you! *(Clasp your hands together.)* **Now I can go in peace, just as Jesus told me to.** *(Stand up and walk in place.)*

LUKE
10:25-37

THEME:
God wants us to help others.

SUMMARY:
Use this SERVICE PROJECT to help children focus on serving others in their churches and communities.

PREPARATION: You'll need Bibles, different colors of construction paper, tape, markers, and scissors.

Help children form pairs, being sure to pair readers with non-readers. Then have children number off from one to two within their pairs. Have the ones read aloud Luke 10:25-32 and the twos read aloud Luke 10:33-37.

In their pairs, have children discuss various service projects they could undertake to serve others in their churches or communities. Some ideas include taking out the trash for an elderly neighbor, doing yardwork for someone who's been ill, or spending time with a shut-in church member.

After each pair has thought of a way to serve others, have it share the idea with the rest of the class. Then give each pair two sheets of construction paper in different colors, a marker, and a pair of scissors.

On one sheet of paper, have a child in each pair trace around his or her left hand. On the other sheet of paper, have the second child trace his or her right hand. Then have kids cut out their handprints. On one handprint, have each pair write their service idea. On the other handprint, have the pair sign their names.

Tape the pairs of handprints to a wall in the lobby of your church as a way to "advertise" the projects the children want to undertake. Let your congregation know that the children in your class want to help them or someone they know.

Children will have fun working in pairs, and the members of your church will enjoy getting to know your young volunteers. After the children have finished the projects written on their handprints, have them add the dates the tasks were accomplished.

LUKE
10:38-42

THEME:
God wants us to make time for him.

SUMMARY:
In this active DEVOTION, children choose between doing busywork and listening to an important message.

PREPARATION: You'll need a Bible, dust rags, peanut butter, plastic knives, saltine crackers, a paper plate, and napkins.

Before class, set up three stations in different areas of your room. At the first station, set out dust rags or scraps of material. At the second station, set out plastic knives, saltine crackers, peanut butter, and a paper plate. At the third station, set out napkins on a serving table.

EXPERIENCE

As children arrive, have them form three groups: the Cleaners, the Cookers, and the Servers. Say: **Today I have an important story to tell you. But the room is such a mess; we really should clean it up. And I have a snack to serve, but it's not ready yet. There's just so much to do!**

Suggest that kids work while you tell the story. Have the Cleaners go to the first station and then use the dust rags to wipe off all of the table tops and desks in the room. Have the Cookers go to the second station, spread peanut butter on crackers, and set the snacks on a paper plate. Have the Servers go to the third station and use napkins to carry individual crackers back to the serving table.

As kids work, quietly tell the story of Mary and Martha from Luke 10:38-42. Keep talking softly until kids have finished their tasks. If the children's tasks take longer than the Bible story, tell the children that Mary and Martha were friends of Jesus and that they lived in Bethany, which is not far from Jerusalem. Explain that these women had a brother named Lazarus, who is mentioned in another part of the Bible and who became a participant in one of Jesus' most famous miracles. Tell the children more about how Jesus brought Lazarus back to life if the children are still working.

RESPONSE

After the children have finished working, call everyone together, and have children sit in a circle. Ask:

■ **What was I talking about while you were working?**

■ **Could you understand everything that I said? Why or why not?**

■ **Why was it hard to listen to me while you worked?**

■ **How is that like being too busy to listen to God in real life?**

Read aloud Luke 10:38-42. Then ask:

■ **What kinds of things distract you from paying attention to God?**

■ **What does Jesus mean when he says, "Only one thing is important"?**

■ **How can you make more time in your life to learn about God?**

CLOSING

Have children form pairs. Say: **Tell your partner one way you'll make time for God this week.** After a few moments, have volunteers share what their partners said. Then close in prayer, asking God to help each child in your class accomplish the goal of making more time for him.

LUKE
11:1-4, 9-10

THEME:
We can pray as Jesus taught us to.

SUMMARY:
In this SKIT, kids read the Lord's Prayer from Luke, chapter 11, and explore what it means to them.

TEACH US TO PRAY

SCENE: Readers are sitting, standing, or kneeling.

PROPS: You'll need to photocopy this skit for the audience members so they can read their part.

CHARACTERS:
You'll need five readers and the audience.

SCRIPT

Reader 1: *(Verse 1a)* One time Jesus was praying in a certain place. When he finished, one of his followers said to him,

Reader 2: *(Verse 1b)* "Lord, teach us to pray as John taught his followers."

Reader 1: *(Verse 2a)* Jesus said to them, "When you pray, say:

Audience: *(Verse 2b)* 'Father, may your name always be kept holy.'"

Reader 3: *(Excitedly)* God, you're so awesome!

Reader 4: Lord, thanks for being in control of everything. You're so powerful in my life!

Reader 5: *(Smiling)* God, you're really neat! I love talking to you.

Audience: *(Verse 2c)* "'May your kingdom come.'"

Reader 1: *(Amazed)* Lord, you're so powerful; one day, everyone will bow down before you!

Reader 3: I can't wait till things here are like they are in heaven. Heaven must be so cool!

Reader 5: Someday we'll know what heaven's like.

Audience: *(Verse 3)* "'Give us the food we need for each day.'"

Reader 2: *(Kneeling)* Lord, you know about the need my family has ...

Reader 4: *(Sadly)* Heal my mom. She's so sick.

Reader 1: Please, Lord, help my dad find a good job.

Audience: *(Verse 4a)* "'Forgive us for our sins ...'"

Reader 3: *(Looking down)* I'm sorry I lied to my teacher, God.

Reader 5: *(With open hands)* Lord, please forgive me for taking that book from my friend.

Reader 2: God, I know you heard that bad word I said. Please forgive me.

Audience: *(Verse 4b)* "'... because we forgive everyone who has done wrong to us.'"

Reader 4: Thanks for my great friends.

Reader 1: I'm glad you gave me such a super family!

Reader 5: God, thanks for helping my cousin and me make up after our fight.

Audience: *(Verse 4c)* "'And do not cause us to be tempted.'"

Reader 2: Lord, please help me not to say bad words when I'm mad.

Reader 3: God, help me keep my eyes on my own paper during this week's test.

Reader 4: Lord, please give me the strength to say no when my friends want to do something wrong.

Audience: *(Verse 9)* So I tell you, ask, and God will give to you. Search, and you will find. Knock, and the door will open for you.

Reader 1: *(Kneeling, bowing head)* God, help me.

Reader 2: *(Kneeling, folding hands)* Lord, thank you.

Reader 3: *(Kneeling, looking up, and holding arms out)* Jesus, I need you.

Audience: *(verse 10)* Yes, everyone who asks will receive. The one who searches will find. And everyone who knocks will have the door opened.

If you use this skit as a discussion starter, here are possible questions:

■ **Why is prayer so important?**

■ **How does prayer help in each part of your life?**

■ **How do you think God feels when you take time to pray?**

■ **Why is each part of the Lord's Prayer so special?**

LUKE 11:5-10

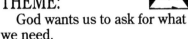

THEME:

God wants us to ask for what we need.

SUMMARY:

In this active DEVOTION, children must figure out that if they ask for snacks, they'll receive them.

PREPARATION: You'll need a Bible and several snacks, such as bowls of popcorn or plates of cookies.

EXPERIENCE

Before class, place the snacks in a prominent place, but do not refer to them. Have the children stand shoulder to shoulder at one end of the room while you stand at the other end. Play a game of Mother, May I? with the children, giving them permission to take baby steps, giant steps, scissors steps, bunny steps, crab steps, or bear steps.

To make the game more challenging for older kids, have each find a partner, stand back to back, link arms, and then follow the directions as they move together as one person.

RESPONSE

After the game, have children sit in a circle with you. Ask:

■ **When were you allowed to move during our game?**

■ **Why did some of you have to go back to the starting line?**

As children answer your questions, help yourself to small portions of the snack. If any of the children ask to share the snack, offer them a portion without making a comment. Offer the snack to anyone who asks.

Then read aloud Luke 11:5-10.

■ **How did the man in the story get what he wanted?**

■ **What does the Bible say will happen to everyone who asks?**

CLOSING

Say: **I brought this snack today for all of us to share. I've just been waiting for you to ask. Is anyone hungry?** When the children ask, freely distribute the snack. As they enjoy the treat, reread Luke 11:5-10.

Close by praying: **Thank you, God, for promising to answer us when we ask. Help us to always come to you with our needs. In Jesus' name, amen.**

LUKE
12:22-31

THEME:
God will provide for us.

SUMMARY:
Use this SKIT to help kids realize that God takes care of his creation.

A BIRD'S-EYE VIEW

SCENE: Several birds are sitting in a nest in a tree.

PROPS: You'll need gummy worms, a space heater, newspaper, a bag of potato chips, knitting needles, yarn, and a long table set on its side with crepe paper taped to it to resemble a nest. You may wish to tape craft feathers or construction paper feathers to the arms and tummies of the characters.

CHARACTERS:
Cindy Sparrow (nervous and worried)
Roy Robin (calm and happy)
Audience Owls (the rest of the class)

SCRIPT

(Each time the Audience Owls hear Roy Robin tell a way God cares for birds, the Owls call out, "Who? Who?" as they flap their arms like wings. Each time, Roy Robin turns toward the audience to answer.)

(Cindy Sparrow is fussing and fiddling inside her nest. She pulls out a space heater and looks around for an outlet to plug it into.)

Cindy Sparrow: Oh! Why don't they wire these trees with electricity? How am I supposed to plug in my heater? Hmm... maybe I need an extension cord. *(Rummages around in nest.)*

Roy Robin: *("Flies" in and sits in the nest.)* Cindy Sparrow, what are you doing? *(Pointing to the heater)* What is that thing?

Cindy: Hi, Roy Robin. It's a space heater, and I'm going to use it in my nest this winter. It'll keep me toasty warm; the only problem is that I don't know where to plug it in!

Roy: A space heater? Birds don't use heaters! *(Pats arms and tummy.)* God gave us these downy feathers to keep us warm.

Audience Owls: Who? Who?

Roy: *(Turns toward audience.)* God!

Cindy: Feathers... ha! These flimsy things won't keep me warm—as if this nest isn't bad enough!

Roy: *(Looks around the nest.)* What's wrong with this nest? It's one of the best around.

Cindy: This straw is so weak! It'll blow away at the first strong wind. And then where will I be? Actually, I've been thinking about this... *(Pulls out a newspaper and motions to a particular ad.)*

Roy: A condominium? Are you kidding? God protects us in our nests.

Audience Owls: Who? Who?

Roy: *(Turns toward audience.)* God! He's taught us how to make them strong enough to outlast just about any storm. Why would you want to live in a condo?

Cindy: Well, I'm just worried that my nest will fall apart. And I don't want to shiver the winter away, either.

Roy: You may be falling apart, but your nest is fine! God's always looked after us, and he's looking after us right now, too.

Audience Owls: Who? Who?

Roy: *(Turns toward audience.)* God!

Cindy: *(Pulls out a bag of potato chips and munches a few chips. Talking with her mouth full)* I know, it's just that—mmm, these are good!

Roy: *(Grabs the bag from Cindy.)* What are these?

Cindy: Potato chips, you birdbrain! Want some?

Roy: Birds don't eat potato chips! God provides delicious worms and seeds for us.

Audience Owls: Who? Who?

Roy: *(Turns toward audience.)* God! *(Pulls a gummy worm from his pocket, dangles it in the air, then eats it.)* Why would you buy potato chips?

Cindy: Well, in case I can't find worms. You never know when worms will run out!

Roy: *(Slaps his forehead.)* Can't you trust God for anything? He always provides for us.

Audience Owls: Who? Who?

Roy: *(Turns toward audience.)* God! I mean, look at the flowers over there. *(Points offstage.)* Aren't they beautiful?

Cindy: *(Shrugs.)* Yeah, I guess so. *(Goes back to rummaging in her nest.)*

Roy: Well, you don't see them moving into a greenhouse or buying plant food or dying their petals do you? God takes care of them just as he cares for us.

Audience Owls: Who? Who?

Roy: *(Turns toward audience.)* God!

Cindy: *(Not listening, rummaging through her nest)* Huh? Oh yeah, the flowers are pretty. I wonder where they get the dye for their petals? Ah-ha! *(Pulls out knitting needles and yarn.)* Here they are!

Roy: What are those, Cindy?

Cindy: Knitting needles, Roy Robin. I'm making myself a winter sweater. I'm no birdbrain! I'm gonna be warm this winter. *(Begins to "knit.")*

(Roy looks at audience, slaps his forehead, then shakes his head.)

If you use this skit as a discussion starter, here are possible questions:

■ **What things do we worry about?**

■ **Is it foolish to worry? Why?**

■ **How can we trust God to provide for us?**

■ **When you look at the way God takes care of the birds and flowers, how does that make you feel?**

■ **What can you trust God to provide for you?**

LUKE 14:7-11

THEME:
God wants us to be humble.

SUMMARY:
Use this LEARNING GAME to help children understand the concept of humility.

PREPARATION: You'll need a Bible, chairs, and snacks. You'll also need a cassette player and a tape of favorite praise music.

Before this activity, set up a simple obstacle course using chairs. Let the ages and maturity level of your children determine how difficult to make the course. Place the snack on a table at the end of the obstacle course.

Read aloud Luke 14:7-11. Then say: **Let's pretend I've invited you to a big party at my house. We'll play a fun game to get there.**

Have children crawl, rather than walk, around the chairs from one end of the room to the other. As children crawl, play the tape of praise music.

After all the children have arrived at the end of the course, ask them how it felt to crawl, rather than walk, through the course. Say: **The word "humble" comes from a Latin word that means "low" or "close to the ground." In the game we just played, I invited everyone to crawl through the obstacle course. In our Bible story, the host of the party chose the most humble person to come sit in a more important place. If we humble ourselves before God, he'll make us great.**

Invite the children to share the snack you set out at the end of the obstacle course. Then close with high fives and a group cheer praising God's goodness!

LUKE
14:12-14

THEME:
God welcomes everyone.

SUMMARY:
Use this PARTY to help kids celebrate God's love and pass that love on to others.

PREPARATION: You'll need a Bible and party supplies as described below for the activities you choose to do.

To celebrate God's love for everyone, have a dress-up party. Meet kids at the door with dress-up clothes and face paint. Invite kids to dress up like the many different kinds of people God welcomes into his kingdom.

To develop the point of the Bible passage, explain that people who are poor, unpopular, poorly dressed, or strangers are welcome at this party. You might want to provide torn or out-of-style clothing for dress-up, face paints and eyebrow pencils to make dirty faces, and strips of material to make bandages or slings.

As kids are dressing up, read aloud Luke 14:12-14. Say: **It's good news that everyone is invited to God's party—even those of us who are sometimes unpopular, who feel left out, who are scared or sick or hurting.**

Say: **Everyone's invited to God's banquet! Let's celebrate!**

Play games in which everyone looks clumsy, such as Twister or sack races, or play games that involve someone being left out, such as Musical Chairs or Monkey in the Middle.

Then say: **These types of games can make us feel awkward or isolated. But God wants everyone to become part of his family. We're all welcome!** Ask:

■ **What kinds of situations make you feel awkward in real life?**

■ **How does knowing that God loves you help you in those situations?**

You could also include give-away games in your celebration. In give-away games, the object of the game is to give away more than you keep. Give each child ten beans; then tell children they'll have three minutes to give away all of their beans. They may only give away their beans one at a time, and if others offer them beans, they must accept them.

As a snack, serve "dirt dessert." Mash chocolate sandwich cookies, and place the crumbs at the bottom of cups. Then spoon chocolate pudding over the ground-up cookies. For an extra surprise, place a gummy worm near the bottom of each cup.

Provide markers, glue, glitter, and construction paper. Have children make invitations to church activities to give to others. Encourage the children to give the invitations to people other than their close friends.

End the party by thanking God for inviting us all into his kingdom. Ask God to help others get to know him better.

LUKE
15:8-10

THEME:
We are valuable to God.

SUMMARY:
Use this AFFIRMATION ACTIVITY to show children that they are special to God.

PREPARATION: You'll need a Bible, a quarter, large paper circles, pens, and colored markers.

Have the children form a circle. Pass a quarter around the circle, and tell children to look at the profile on the "heads" side of the coin. Tell the children that they're going to create coins decorated with their own profiles.

Give each child a paper circle and a pen, and provide colored markers. Have each child draw a self-profile on one side of his or her paper coin. For extra fun, use a bright light near a wall so children can create shadow profiles to copy.

Encourage children to make their profiles distinctive by adding hair and eye color and other special features.

As children draw, read aloud Luke 15:8-10. Explain that the woman sought the lost coin because it was valuable. Say: **The coins you're making represent you. They're valuable because you're valuable to God.**

After children have finished detailing their coins, have them write their names above their profiles. Then have children pass the coins to the left. Each person will write an affirmation on the back of the coin he or she receives. The affirmation should describe the person whose name is on the front of the coin. Children might write, "You are a good friend" or "You always make people feel welcome in our class." Young children may prefer to write one word describing the person, and they may need help with spelling.

Have children keep passing the coins around the circle until each child receives his or her own coin again. Then collect the coins, and pile them in the center of the circle.

Have children take turns retrieving their coins. Then say: **You were able to find your coin because it was one of a kind, just like you. God made you that way. Just as the coin was special to the woman in the story, you are special to God!**

Let children take their coins home to remind them of how special they are to God.

LUKE
15:11-32

THEME:
God's love never ends.

SUMMARY:
Use this CRAFT idea to demonstrate that God's love is continuous and can't be broken.

PREPARATION: You'll need Bibles, a two-by-fourteen-inch strip of paper as a model, a similar strip for each person, a few staplers, scissors, and pens.

Have several volunteers read aloud Luke 15:11-32. Then say: **Even though the younger son made unwise choices, his father welcomed him home.** Emphasize that there was nothing the son could do that would make his father stop loving him.

Show the class the model strip of paper. Say: **Today we're going to make something that will help us remember that God's love for us goes on and on and can't be broken.** Explain that you are going to make something called a Möbius (MA-be-us) strip. Bring the ends of the paper together as if to join them into a circle, then twist one of the ends a half-twist and staple the ends together twice, once on each edge.

Say: **Now watch. I'm going to cut the strip in half.** Place the tip of your scissors between the staples and under one edge of the paper where the edges meet. Start cutting down the middle of the strip. Keep cutting until you reach your starting point. Show the children that you now have one large, continuous loop.

Give each child a paper strip, and help children make their own Möbius strips.

While children work, talk about how cutting the strip didn't break the loop, just as nothing can break God's love for us. Ask questions such as "How does God show his love for you?" and "Will God ever stop loving you? Why not?"

After kids have finished cutting, distribute pens. Have children write, "God loves me!" again and again along the loop until the words meet. Younger children could draw a series of hearts.

Close in prayer, thanking God for his continuous love for us. Encourage the children to take their Möbius strips home and hang them in prominent spots as reminders of God's love for them.

LUKE 16:19-31

THEME:
We can reach out to others.

SUMMARY:
In this SERVICE PROJECT idea, children commit to helping others in their community.

PREPARATION: You'll need a Bible and a large map of your city or area. You'll also need a blindfold, colored stars, tacks or markers, index cards, and pens.

Before class, place colored stars on the map at the locations of local human-services agencies. Draw a key at the bottom of the map explaining which colored star represents which agency.

When kids arrive, ask volunteers to read aloud Luke 16:19-31. Say: **You've all heard the expression "It was right under my nose." Well poor Lazarus was right under the rich man's nose, but the rich man didn't help him. I'll bet** there are lots of people in our town who are "right under our noses" and need our help.

Have kids form pairs to take turns playing a version of Blind Man's Bluff. Have pairs line up in front of the map. Have each pair choose one person from the pair to be blindfolded; the other person will be the Spinner. As each pair comes to the front of the line, the Spinner will blindfold his or her partner and will slowly spin the blindfolded partner three times. Then the blindfolded partner will place a tack somewhere on the map. If you have younger children in your class, use markers instead of tacks.

Have the blindfolded child remove the blindfold as the Spinner finds the community agency closest to the tack. Tell the pair what that agency does to help others in the community. Then give the pair an index card and pen, and ask the pair to find a spot in the room to brainstorm about ways to help the people served by that agency.

When everyone is finished brainstorming, have pairs share their ideas with the rest of the class. Have each pair circle the idea on their index card that they'd like to try and then tack the index card near the appropriate agency on the map.

After kids have accomplished their goals, have them sign their index cards and write the date they finished their service project. Throw a party after all the cards have been signed to celebrate the helping hands and hearts in your class!

LUKE
18:9-14

THEME:
God knows our hearts.

SUMMARY:
Use this CREATIVE STORYTELL-ING idea to help kids think critically about God's values for us.

PREPARATION: You'll need a Bible, a blackboard, and chalk.

Before class, write the numbers one through five down the left side of the blackboard, separating the numbers by five or six inches. Above the numbers, write the heading, "Pharisee." On the right side of the board, write the same set of numbers under the heading, "Tax Collector."

As kids arrive, have them sit in a circle. Say: **Today we're going to hear about two very different men and the way they talked to God.** Read aloud Luke 18:9-10. Point to the blackboard and explain that you will read part of the Bible story and then will stop to ask questions. The class will "vote" on the answers to your questions by giving a thumbs up or a thumbs down.

Read Luke 18:11-12 aloud. Ask:

■ **Do you think the Pharisee is telling the truth about himself? Why or why not?** (Tally the class's vote by counting the number of thumbs ups and thumbs downs. Write the class's answer next to the number one in the Pharisee column.)

■ **Do you think the Pharisee is a good person? Why or why not?** (Again, tally the vote; then write the class's answer next to the number two in the Pharisee column.)

■ **Is this Pharisee being honest before God? Explain.** (Write the class's answer next to the number three in the Pharisee column.)

■ **Would you want this Pharisee as a friend? Why or why not?** (Write the class's answer next to the number four in the Pharisee column.)

■ **Do you think God knows what this man is really like on the inside? Explain.** (Write the class's answer next to the number five in the Pharisee column.)

Then read Luke 18:13. Ask the same questions about the tax collector that you asked about the Pharisee. Record the answers on the blackboard in the Tax Collector column.

Tally the scores under each heading, and ask volunteers to share their impressions of the two men in the Bible story. Then say: **Now let's see what Jesus says about these two men.**

Read aloud Luke 18:14. Close in prayer, thanking God for seeing us as we really are and asking him to help us to always be honest before him.

LUKE 23:33-46; 24:1-8

THEME:
Jesus is alive!

SUMMARY:
Use this SKIT to teach children the significance of Jesus' death and resurrection. Have kids form groups of five, and let groups act out the skit simultaneously, adapting the characters to fit the group.

THE BEST ASSIGNMENT

SCENE: Angels are hurrying to the empty tomb.

PROPS: You'll need a "Tomb" (a sturdy table covered with a white bedsheet).

CHARACTERS:
Angie (dressed in white)
Albert (dressed in white)
Jesus' friends (three girls in sandals with shawls or large towels wrapped around their shoulders)

SCRIPT

Angie: *(Entering excitedly from offstage)* Hurry up, Albert! Angels can't be late! This is the best assignment we've ever had, and you're gonna blow it!

Albert: *(Enters, yawning.)* Slow down, Angie! It's so early in the morning, and that long trip from heaven was tiring. Maybe we can catch a few winks before the women arrive at the tomb.

Angie: Sleep? How can you possibly sleep at a time like this?

Albert: I was up all night, remember? These double shifts are exhausting.

Angie: *(Looking around)* Well, here we are. The tomb! *(Lifts sheet to peek inside.)* The empty tomb! Boy, are Jesus' friends going to be surprised! *(Claps.)*

Albert: *(Smiling)* I know! I can't wait to see the looks on their faces when they realize that he's conquered death and is alive. Humans are so funny, aren't they?

Angie: *(Nodding)* Yep. *(Giggles.)* Remember the shepherds when we told them about Jesus' birth?

Albert: *(Laughs.)* Their jaws dropped! *(Drops jaw.)* Their eyes got huge! *(Opens eyes wide.)* They about jumped out of their sandals in surprise! *(Runs around excitedly.)*

Angie: And when they went to Bethlehem to see the tiny Savior…well…it was almost like they knew they were looking at God.

Albert: *(Shakes head.)* Yeah, but so few people really knew that he is God's Son. It's really sad, Angie. People didn't even realize that Jesus came because God loves them so much.

Angie: *(Softly)* The same people that Jesus came to save nailed him to a cross and let him die.

Albert: I don't understand it, either. I mean, God loved people enough to send his precious Son to save them from sin. And they didn't even realize it. *(Excitedly)* But Jesus won over death. What a showdown!

Angie: Yeah! Jesus showed that his power is greater than anything! When he conquered death and rose again, he took all those sins with him. *(Imitating an umpire)* They're outta here!

Albert: Oh, and remember when—

Angie: Shh, it's time! They're coming!

(Giggling, the angels stand on the table. Then they look very serious. Jesus' three friends enter, crying and looking sad.)

Albert: Why are you looking for a living person in this place for the dead? He is not here; he has risen from the dead.

Angie: Do you remember what he told you in Galilee? He said the Son of Man must be handed over to sinful people, be crucified, and rise from the dead on the third day.

(Jesus' friends stare at the angels, then at each other. Then the friends break into smiles.)

Jesus' friends: Let's run to tell the others! Let's tell them that Jesus is alive!

Albert: I love this job.

(Albert and Angie give each other high fives, then head offstage.)

If you use this skit as a discussion starter, here are possible questions:

∎ **Why was Jesus' death and resurrection so important?**

∎ **What happened when Jesus conquered death?**

∎ **How do you feel when you remember that God loved you so much that he sent Jesus to die for you?**

∎ **How can you show God your love?**

LUKE
23:39-43

THEME:
Jesus forgives us when we ask.

SUMMARY:
In this creative PRAYER, children discover the parts of a prayer of repentance.

PREPARATION: You'll need Bibles; nice paper in varied colors; glue sticks; pens; and precut, colored cardboard mats to use as borders for the paper. (These can be simply and inexpensively made from poster board.)

Ask a volunteer to read aloud Luke 23:39-43. Then have children form pairs, and give each pair a Bible. Say: **One of the criminals who was crucified with Jesus was forgiven for his sins and went to be with Jesus in heaven.**

Then say: **Study this scene with your partner, and see if you can come up with three important things the criminal said.**

Let children study and discuss the passage for several minutes. (Younger kids may need help.) Then ask each pair to act out one of their three guesses. Let the rest of the class guess what each pair is acting out. Especially acknowledge pairs who come up with any of the following:

1. Jesus is God.
2. I have done wrong.
3. Jesus, remember (forgive) me.

Give children pens, and let them write the three elements of this prayer of repentance on paper. They can then glue the mats to the papers to make framed "models" of a repentance prayer that they can take home and hang in their rooms.

Close with a prayer of repentance. Have each person silently think of something he or she has done wrong. Then pray: **Jesus, thank you for loving us enough to die on the cross for our sins. Thank you for forgiving us when we ask. Amen.**

LUKE
24:1-12

THEME:
Jesus rose from the dead.

SUMMARY:
Use this CRAFT project to remind children of the surprise the women must have felt when they saw the stone rolled away from Jesus' tomb.

PREPARATION: You'll need Bibles, paper cups, twelve-inch lengths of string, sharpened pencils, and aluminum foil.

Have several volunteers read Luke 24:1-12 aloud. Tell children that they're going to make a craft that will remind them of how the stone was rolled away from Jesus' tomb.

Distribute a paper cup, a length of string, a pencil, and a three-by-three-inch square of aluminum foil to each child. Show children how to use the sharpened pencil to poke a small hole in the bottom of the cup. Then thread the string through the hole and tie a knot on the end of the string inside the cup so the string won't pull through.

Next, wrap the sheet of aluminum foil around the other end of the string and crumple the foil into a ball. Show children how to catch the foil ball inside the cup.

Explain that the tomb where Jesus was buried was probably one of the cave-like tombs common at that time. Show children that when the ball is in the cup, it looks like the stone that covered the entrance to the tomb. Then show children that when the ball is out of the cup, the cup is empty—just as the tomb was!

Encourage children to take home their craft projects and to remember—every time they play with the toys–that Jesus rose from the dead.

LUKE 24:36-45

THEME:
Jesus is real!

SUMMARY:
In this QUIET REFLECTION, children think about Jesus' appearance to the disciples after his crucifixion.

PREPARATION: You'll need a Bible, an instant camera, enough film to take one more photo than there are children in your class, and a snack such as a bowl of popcorn.

Ask a volunteer to read aloud Luke 24:36-45. Then group children together and take a class picture with an instant camera. Have children quickly sit in a circle, and pass the developing picture around for the children to observe. Ask:

■ **What is starting to happen to the picture?**

■ **Can you tell what it is yet?**

■ **Why can't we see all of the picture's details right away?**

Reread Luke 24:36-45. Then pass the developed picture around the circle again. Ask:

■ **Can you recognize who's in the picture now?**

Say: **Just as we had trouble recognizing the people in the picture right away, Jesus' disciples had trouble recognizing him until he had spent time with them and explained his resurrection. Today, we have the disciples' witness in the Bible to show us that Jesus is real!**

Have kids line up, and take a picture of each student in your class. Say: **Your picture is of someone Jesus recognizes and loves— you! Take your photo home to remind you that Jesus is real and that his love for you is real, too!**

JOHN

"God loved the world so much that he gave his one and only Son so that whoever believes in him may not be lost, but have eternal life."

John 3:16

JOHN 1:1-9

THEME:
Jesus is the light of the world.

SUMMARY:
In this OBJECT LESSON, kids discover how the light of Jesus can never be put out.

PREPARATION: You'll need a Bible, a flashlight, matches, and re-lighting candles.

This activity works best with older children.

Lead the children into a darkened room, have them form a circle, and read John 1:1-9 by flashlight.

Distribute relighting candles to each person, then use a match to light your candle. Use your candle to light the candle of the person to your right. As you light the candle, have everyone say, "Jesus is the light of the world." Have the children pass the flame around the circle until everyone has a lit candle. Each time a new candle is lit, have everyone say, "Jesus is the light of the world!"

After all the candles are lit, allow group members to call out things that can weaken the light of Christ, such as lying, stealing, and saying bad words. Each time children mention something, have them all try to blow out their candles. Children will be delighted to see their candles flicker but then blaze back up. When children run out of ideas, close in prayer, thanking God that the light of Jesus can never be put out.

JOHN
1:35-46

THEME:
We're called to follow Jesus.

SUMMARY:
On this field TRIP, kids experience what it might have been like to be a follower of Jesus long ago.

PREPARATION: You'll need Bibles, envelopes, a pencil or pen, five slips of paper, and refreshments.

Before this activity, write the following clues on slips of paper, omitting the location in parentheses.

∎ Clue 1: Read John 2:1-11. Jesus performed a miracle, didn't he? Now hurry to the place where a wedding might be! (The sanctuary.)

∎ Clue 2: Read John 4:4-14. Jesus' living water set the sad woman free. Now go get a drink, and find Clue 3! (A drinking fountain.)

∎ Clue 3: Read John 6:5-13. Jesus fed a crowd with five loaves and two fish. Where might you go to enjoy a tasty dish? (The kitchen.)

∎ Clue 4: Read John 18:1. Jesus went to a garden with some of his friends. When you find this garden, your treasure hunt will end. (A tree, flower bed, or garden.)

Set Clue 1 aside, then place each clue in a colorful envelope. Place each envelope beside a Bible in the appropriate location in your church. For example, tape the envelope containing Clue 2 in a visible place in your sanctuary. Then set up a refreshment table in a garden or near a flower bed.

Gather the children together, and explain that they're going on an adventure. Read Clue 1 aloud, and have children walk to the sanctuary to find Clue 2. Have children work together to figure out where the next clue might be. As you walk to each location, ask questions such as "What do you think it was like for the disciples to follow Jesus everywhere?" and "How are we like the disciples?"

When children reach the refreshments, allow them to enjoy the treats. Read aloud John 1:35-46, then ask:

∎ **Why did the disciples want to follow Jesus?**

∎ **What did they give up to follow Jesus?**

∎ **Why do you want to follow Jesus?**

∎ **What do we give up when we follow Jesus?**

Close in prayer, asking God to help us be his faithful followers.

JOHN
2:1-11

THEME:
Jesus can do anything.

SUMMARY:
In this active DEVOTION, children reenact what happened at Jesus' first miracle.

PREPARATION: You'll need a Bible; paper cups; water; red, presweetened drink mix; and two or three nontransparent pitchers.

Before this activity, put a package of red, presweetened drink mix in the bottom of each container.

EXPERIENCE

Read John 2:1-11 aloud, and have a few volunteers fill the containers with water. Then have a few other volunteers pour a cup of "water" for each person in class. Children will be surprised when the water turns out to be punch!

RESPONSE

As kids enjoy their punch, ask:

■ **What was your reaction when the water came out red?**

■ **How was this activity like Jesus turning the water to wine? How was it different?**

■ **How do you think the guests and disciples reacted when Jesus turned water to wine?**

■ **Why do you think Jesus performed a miracle at the wedding?**

■ **What miracles does God perform today?**

CLOSING

Pray: **Dear God, thank you for sending Jesus to show your power and take our sins away. Help us look to you for help in every situation. Amen.**

JOHN 3:16-17

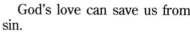

THEME:

God's love can save us from sin.

SUMMARY:

In this AFFIRMATION ACTIVITY, children learn that God sent Jesus to save us because he loves us.

PREPARATION: You'll need a Bible, a skateboard, masking tape, and an eight-foot length of sturdy rope.

Use a masking tape line to divide your classroom in half. Form two groups, and send each group to a different side of the room. Give the skateboard to one group and the rope to the second group.

Say: **The members of the first group are drowning in a stormy sea. The people in the second group are the Lifesavers. They'll use the rope to pull the members of the drowning group to safety.**

Have the Lifesavers gather together and toss one end of the rope to the first member of the drowning group. Instruct that person to grasp the end of the rope and sit on the skateboard while the Lifesavers pull him or her to their side. As the person is being pulled, have the Lifesavers say encouraging phrases such as "You're almost here!" "We're glad you finally made it!" or "I'm glad we got to save you!" After the child crosses the line, have him or her get off the skateboard and push it back to the drowning group. Encourage the Lifesavers to give high fives and pats on the back to each person they save.

When each member of the drowning group has been saved, have groups switch roles and play again. Then form a circle and read John 3:16-17 aloud. Ask:

■ **What was it like to be pulled to safety?**

■ **How does God save us?**

■ **What does God save us from?**

■ **Why does God save us?**

■ **How does it feel to know that God loves you enough to send his Son to die for you?**

love is like this baking soda— nothing special. That's what the woman at the well felt like before she met Jesus. But after she met Jesus . . . (pour the vinegar into the glass jar, and watch the bubbly reaction) . . . **her life had joy and meaning and excitement! She was bubbling over with happiness!**

Ask:

■ **How does Jesus' love change your life?**

■ **How do you feel when you think about how much Jesus loves you?**

■ **Who can you share your "bubbly" excitement with?**

JOHN 4:3-30

THEME:
God's love gives us abundant life.

SUMMARY:
Use this OBJECT LESSON to help children understand that God's love and forgiveness bring peace and joy to our lives.

PREPARATION: You'll need a Bible, one tablespoon of baking soda, one-third cup of vinegar, and a glass jar.

Have the children form a circle, and place the glass jar in the middle. Read John 4:3-30 aloud. Then pour the baking soda in the jar and say: **Life without God's**

JOHN 6:5-14

THEME:
God provides for us.

SUMMARY:
Kids will enjoy this active DEVOTION as they discover ways God provides for them in their daily lives.

PREPARATION: You'll need a Bible, a cassette of praise music, a cassette player, paper cups, and a dinner roll for each child. Children should wash their hands before this activity.

EXPERIENCE
Distribute the dinner rolls and paper cups, then say: **When I start the music, tear off a piece of your roll and give it to someone**

nearby. As you do, tell that person something God has given you such as a home, food, a family, friends, good teachers, or warm clothes. Then move around the room and repeat the activity with each person in the room. When others give you bread, put it in your cup.

Start the music, and encourage children to think of things they might normally take for granted. After a minute or two, turn off the cassette player and form a circle.

RESPONSE
Ask:
■ **What things did people mention?**
■ **Why does God provide so many great things for us?**
Read John 6:5-14 aloud. Then ask:
■ **Why did Jesus provide food for the crowd?**
■ **Why do you think the disciples doubted him?**
■ **Do you ever doubt that God will provide for you? Explain.**

CLOSING
Say: **Look at the cupful of bread you have. Each piece represents something that God has given us out of his love. Just as God gave the extra baskets of food, God gives us more blessings than we could even begin to count. Before we enjoy our snack, let's pray and thank God for all he provides for us.**
Choose a volunteer to close in prayer.

JOHN 8:12

THEME:
Jesus is the light of the world.

SUMMARY:
Use this SKIT to help children understand that Jesus is like a light, guiding them through difficulties.

NIGHT LIGHT

SCENE: Four people are hiking through a dark forest.

PROPS: You'll need a flashlight and three backpacks. Before the skit, have children or people from the audience scatter around the stage as "trees." Turn the lights down or off completely.

CHARACTERS:
Desiree (girl camper with a backpack)
Jack (boy camper with a backpack)
Austin (boy camper with a backpack)
Carlos (park ranger with a flashlight)

SCRIPT
(The scout troop enters, whistling a song.)
Desiree: Hey, it's dark in this forest. Wait, you guys! Are you sure you want to go farther?
Jack: Of course! We have to go through the forest to get to camp. Mr. Donelson's got hot dogs, cold soda, and s'mores waiting for us there. C'mon,

Desiree, let's go.

Austin: I'm with Desiree, Jack. It's dark in here. *(Bumps into a "tree.")* Ow! I think we should go back!

Desiree: I didn't say go back. It's just as dark back there! I think we should sit here and wait until morning.

Jack: In this spooky forest? You're crazy.

Austin: But you'll get lost if you try to go forward.

(All three sit down and wait. Jack sits on a rock; Desiree leans against a tree.)

Desiree: *(Nervously)* What's that noise?

Jack: I heard it, too.

Carlos: *(Enters with a flashlight.)* Hey, kids, what's up?

Austin: *(Suspiciously)* Who are you?

Carlos: I'm a park ranger. Your scout leader, Mr. Donelson, said you'd all forgotten your flashlights and you might be having trouble finding your way back to camp. If you're tired of sitting in the dark, we can head back.

Desiree: I'm sure tired of this creepy forest. Let's go!

Jack: Me, too. I can taste those hot dogs already!

Austin: Wait a minute! Just because some guy shows up with a flashlight saying he's a park ranger, do you believe him?

Desiree: Why not?

Austin: What if his flashlight goes out? Why do you trust him?

Jack: He's the only light we have, Austin. Otherwise, we're lost!

Austin: Well, I'd rather stay lost than follow him. *(Sits down against a rock.)*

Jack: Hey, Austin, don't you re-

member in church last week when we learned that Jesus is the light of the world and that he's with us when we're in trouble? Jesus gives us light so we can follow him. If you ignore the light, you'll stay lost!

Desiree: Yeah, Austin. You want to be *found,* not lost! And Jesus is the light of the world.

(The trees begin whispering, "Jesus is the light. Jesus is the light.")

Carlos: Listen, Austin. Even the wind in the trees knows that Jesus is the light of the world—and the forest!

Austin: *(Thinks for a moment.)* You're right, guys! I do want to follow the light. C'mon, let's go. I'm starving!

(Everyone walks offstage.)

If you use this skit as a discussion starter, here are possible questions:

■ **How did Jesus bring light to the world?**

■ **When do you feel like you're in the dark forest?**

■ **Why do some people choose not to follow Jesus?**

■ **How can you show them the light of Jesus?**

JOHN
8:31-38

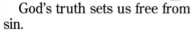

THEME:
God's truth sets us free from sin.

SUMMARY:
In this LEARNING GAME, children learn how sin makes us slaves while God's love sets us free.

PREPARATION: You'll need a Bible, a beanbag, poster board or newsprint, and a marker. Write "sin" on the beanbag. Make a sign that says "Jail," and place it in one corner of the room.

Have the children form a circle and then sit down. Pass the beanbag around the circle as in the game Hot Potato. When you say "stop," have the child holding the beanbag stand up and walk to a corner of the room marked Jail. Continue playing until four children are in jail. Then read John 8:31-38 aloud. Have everyone shout, "God's truth sets us free!" and then skip to the jail to "free" the children there. After playing a few rounds, ask:

■ **What does God's love and truth set us free from?**

■ **How do sins lock us up?**

■ **How can we ask God to free us from sin?**

JOHN
9:1-12

THEME:
Jesus, the great physician, can heal the wounds of our world.

SUMMARY:
In this creative PRAYER, children ask Jesus to heal their world.

PREPARATION: You'll need a Bible, a red marker, a large world-map, plastic bandages, and ball-point pens.

Have the children form a circle, and place the map in the middle of the circle. Briefly talk about places where poverty, war, violence, oppression, abuse, or godlessness abound. Use a red marker to put a dot on each country or area you mention.

Distribute plastic bandages and ballpoint pens. Have each child write a prayer for the world on his or her bandage. Children may write things such as "God, please help the people in China learn about you," or "Jesus, take away the hate and war in Africa."

When children have finished, read John 9:1-12 aloud. Say: **Just as Jesus healed the blind man, he can heal the wounds of our world. Let's pray right now.** Have children take turns reading their prayers and then sticking their bandages to the map. Close by joining hands around the map and praying: **Dear God, we know** we live in a broken world. Please heal the pain and suffering of people in our country and people who are far away. Just as you allowed the blind man to see, allow us to see you heal our world. In Jesus' name, amen.

JOHN 10:1-15

THEME:
Jesus is the good shepherd.

SUMMARY:
Children enjoy a PARTY to celebrate Jesus' leadership.

PREPARATION: Three to four weeks before the party, send out sheep-shaped invitations, and encourage children to come dressed as shepherds. Include the reference "John 10:1-15" on the invitation, and ask children to read the passage before they arrive. You'll need other supplies and ingredients as mentioned in the activities below.

Have children enter the party by using a secret password such as "Baa baa black sheep" or "Mary had a little lamb." Serve shepherd's pie and sheep-shaped sugar cookies that kids can decorate with white frosting and shredded coconut. Games might include...

■ a cotton-ball scavenger hunt. The first group to get "three (sandwich) bags full" wins.

■ a maze toss. Have the children form a circle and toss a ball of fluffy white yarn back and forth, creating a maze. As children toss the yarn to the next person, have them finish the sentence, "God has been a good shepherd to me by..."

■ Hide-and-Seek. Have a "shepherd" search for his or her "lost lambs."

During the party, explain that it's important for sheep to follow their shepherd so they don't get lost or hurt. Sing songs such as "I Have Decided to Follow Jesus" and "The Lord Is My Shepherd."

JOHN 11:17-44

THEME:
We can trust what Jesus says.

SUMMARY:
On this field TRIP, kids experience what it's like to trust a friend.

PREPARATION: You'll need a Bible, bandannas or scarves to use as blindfolds, and a written permission slip signed by a parent or guardian from each child. You'll need to arrange for adults to drive and help out with this field trip. You also might need to get permission from a miniature golf course.

Take children to a miniature golf course, and have them form pairs. Blindfold one partner in each pair, and explain that the other partner must assist the blindfolded partner in walking from hole to hole and in golfing. Tell children that they'll switch roles halfway through the game so everyone will have a chance to be blindfolded. Send small groups of children through the course with an adult. After everyone has finished the course, gather at a park for lunch. Ask:

■ **What was it like to be blindfolded?**

■ **What was it like to help your blindfolded partner?**

Read John 11:17-44, then ask:

■ **Why was it hard for Mary and Martha to believe Jesus?**

Say: **Just as you had to trust your partner, Mary and Martha had to trust Jesus. We can trust Jesus too. When it seems like we're walking in the dark, he'll guide us.**

JOHN 11:35

THEME:
    Jesus understands our feelings.

SUMMARY:
    In this creative PRAYER, kids give their worries and concerns to God.

PREPARATION: You'll need a Bible, facial tissues, an empty tissue box, and pens.

Gather children around you. Distribute tissues and pens and say: **When we're sad, we use tissues to wipe away our tears. On your tissue, write down something that makes you sad or worried.** After the children write their concerns, read John 11:35 aloud. Ask:

■ **What would it be like to see Jesus crying?**

■ **What things make Jesus sad?**

Say: **Jesus was sad that his close friend Lazarus was dead. But Jesus also cried because he knew how sad Lazarus' sisters and friends were. Jesus cares for our hurts, too. Let's pray silently, and as we do, put your tissue in this box and remember that Jesus wants to wipe away your tears.**

Pass around the empty tissue box as the children pray silently, and have the children put their tissues in the box.

JOHN 12:12-16

THEME:
    It's important to praise Jesus.

SUMMARY:
    Use this MUSIC IDEA to help children praise Jesus just as the people of Jerusalem did long ago.

PREPARATION: You'll need a Bible, a cassette or CD player, a palm branch (or a picture of one), and a cassette or CD of the song "Hosanna" by Michael W. Smith.

Read John 12:12-16 aloud, then ask:

■ **What would it have been like in Jerusalem that day?**

Say: **One way we praise God today is through singing. Let's praise God with this song that Michael W. Smith wrote about the day Jesus rode into Jerusalem.**

Have children form a circle and hold hands or link arms. If you have more than ten children, form several circles. Place a palm branch on the floor in front of one person's feet. Have the children walk in a circle as they sing the chorus: "Blessed is he who comes in the name of the Lord, hosanna, hosanna, hosanna." When the chorus is over, stop the cassette. Have the person standing in front of the palm branch tell one thing he or she loves about Jesus such as "I'm glad Jesus died for our sins" or "I think it's neat that God sent his Son as a baby." Then repeat the song's chorus. During the verses, children may sing along, waving their hands on the word "hosanna." Repeat the song and movements until all the children have had an opportunity to praise Jesus.

JOHN 13:2-17

THEME:
Jesus wants us to serve others.

SUMMARY:
Through this SERVICE PROJECT, children experience the joy that comes from secretly serving others.

PREPARATION: You'll need Bibles, scissors, crayons, newspaper, window-washing fluid, and red construction paper.

Form trios, and have one person in each group read John 13:2-17 aloud. Say: **Jesus showed his love by serving his friends in a humble way. Let's show our love by serving those around us today!**

Have trios work together to cut out hearts from red construction paper. Instruct children to write encouraging messages such as "Jesus loves you" or "Have a great day" on each heart. Then send trios into your church parking lot, armed with newspaper, window-washing fluid, and their heart notes. Have kids work together to wash as many car windows as they can in the allotted time, leaving an encouraging note on each clean windshield.

Afterward, gather together and talk about what it was like to serve others.

JOHN
13:34-35

THEME:
Jesus wants us to love one another.

SUMMARY:
In this AFFIRMATION ACTIVITY, children are challenged to encourage each other all month long.

PREPARATION: A few weeks before you begin, make posters saying, "L.O.A. is coming!" Send letters to the children and their parents explaining what you'll be doing. Assign each child the name of another child as an L.O.A. pal.

TEACHER TIP
To avoid the "cootie factor," pair boys with boys and girls with girls.

Explain that this is L.O.A. (Love One Another) Month and that each person has a secret L.O.A. pal. Distribute slips of paper that tell each child who his or her pal will be. Have each child decorate a shoe box to be his or her mailbox. Set the mailboxes together as a mail center where L.O.A. pals can leave encouraging notes, Bible verses, pictures, or small gifts for each other.

Make a banner for your room with John 13:34-35 written on it to encourage kids to remember their L.O.A. pals all month. End the month with a party, and serve heart-shaped cookies decorated with the letters L.O.A. Have kids try to guess who their pals were.

JOHN
14:1-6

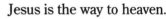

THEME:
Jesus is the way to heaven.

SUMMARY:
For this CRAFT project, children discover how to tell the Gospel story with colorful beads.

PREPARATION: You'll need gray, red, white, green, and yellow craft beads and a ten-inch length of suede lacing for each person. Suede lacing is available at craft stores.

Set out the beads and lacing. Say: **We're going to make a craft that tells people the story of Jesus. The gray beads represent how sin makes our hearts dirty. Red symbolizes the blood that Jesus shed when he died on the cross. White shows that Jesus' death makes us clean and new because he took our sins away. Green reminds us of spring and that we can have new life in Christ. And yellow represents the streets of gold in heaven, where Jesus is preparing a place for us to live.**

Have children use suede lacing to string the beads in the appropriate order, tying a knot before each one. Then have children tie the lacing around their wrists and practice telling each other the Gospel story.

JOHN 14:26

THEME:
The Holy Spirit is our helper.

SUMMARY:
Use this MUSIC IDEA to help kids discover the importance of obeying the Holy Spirit.

PREPARATION: You'll need a Bible, a cassette of the song "When the Spirit Says Move," and a cassette player.

Read John 14:26 aloud. Say: **God sent his Holy Spirit to help us know what things are right and what things are wrong. So when the Holy Spirit tells us what to do, we need to obey.**

Teach children the song "When the Spirit Says Move"; then have them form four groups. Instruct each group to come up with a new motion for the song, such as dance, high five, clap, or sneeze. Then sing the song again, allowing each group to lead the class in doing its motion. Ask:

■ **Why do we need the Holy Spirit?**

■ **What would happen if we didn't have the Holy Spirit?**

■ **How can you thank God for giving us his Holy Spirit?**

Close in prayer, thanking God for the Holy Spirit.

JOHN 15:1-10

THEME:
Jesus wants us to bear spiritual fruit.

SUMMARY:
Use this PARTY to teach children the joy that comes when we bear fruit for Jesus.

PREPARATION: You'll need a Bible and supplies as indicated below.

Two weeks before the party, send out fruit-shaped invitations. Ask each child to bring a different kind of fruit to contribute to a large salad.

As children arrive, allow them to choose an activity from several options. You may have one group making fruit salad (with the supervision of an adult), another group making fruit-shaped name tags, and another group playing Hi-Ho-Cherry-O.

Play games such as...

■ Fruit-Basket Upset. Place chairs in a circle, and have the children sit in the chairs. Instruct each child to secretly choose a fruit name. Then stand in the middle and call out the name of a fruit. Children who've chosen that fruit must change places while you try to take one of their seats. The child left in the middle may call out another fruit name or say, "Fruit-Basket Upset" to have everyone change places.

■ Mystery Orchard. Have children form two groups: the Farmers and the Trees. Have the Farmers leave the room while the Trees decide what strange kind of fruit they grow on their branches—pizzananas, chocolapples, or burritoberries, for example. Then have the Farmers come back and ask questions which have "yes" or "no" answers to try and discover what fruit the Trees produce.

As snacks for the party, serve fruit salad, fruit punch, and dried fruit. Have children bob for apples or dip fruit in chocolate or caramel.

After some fruity fun, gather children around you. Read John 15:1-10 aloud, and explain that Jesus wasn't talking about real fruit. Ask:

■ **What good things happen when we follow Jesus?**

■ **Why do we need Jesus to make those things happen?**

■ **How are these good things like fruit?**

Tell children that Jesus wants us to help others know him, to grow closer to him, and to become more like God each day.

JOHN
18:15-18, 25-27

THEME:
Jesus loves us even when we sin.

SUMMARY:
In this QUIET REFLECTION, children discover that Jesus died to forgive our sins.

PREPARATION: You'll need a Bible.

Have children scatter around the room and sit down. Say: **Peter was one of Jesus' closest friends. That's why Peter was astonished when Jesus said, "Before the rooster crows, you'll deny that you know me three times."**

Read John 18:15-18. Say: **Peter's first denial hurt Jesus. Stand up, and think of a time you've done something that hurt God.** Pause for a few seconds, then read John 18:25. Say: **Peter's second denial hurt Jesus, too. Stretch out your right arm as if it were nailed to a cross. Now think of a time you've hurt a friend.** Pause for a few seconds, then read John 18:26-27. Say: **Jesus was right when he said Peter would turn against him three times. Stretch out your left arm as if it's nailed to a cross. Think of a time you've hurt someone in your family.** Pause for a few seconds.

Say: **Listen as I read John 3:16-17. Each time you hear the word "Son," cross one of your arms across your chest.** After you read John 3:16-17, children will be standing with their arms crossed over their chests. Say: **Now you're making the sign for love. Jesus died to show us his love. Jesus' forgiveness takes away those bad, hurtful things we've done.**

To close, lead the children in prayer. Pray: **Dear God, thank you for sending Jesus and for allowing him to die to take away our sins. Help us trust and follow Jesus and remember how painful sins can be. In Jesus' name, amen.**

JOHN
19:16-30;
19:38-20:18

THEME:
Jesus' bore our sins when he died on the cross.

SUMMARY:
In this CRAFT project, children think about the pain Jesus chose to go through so we could have eternal life.

PREPARATION: You'll need a Bible, two four-inch nails per child, six-inch lengths of thin-gauge wire, and twelve-inch lengths of leather lacing.

Distribute the nails, then read John 19:16-30 aloud. Explain that when Jesus died, he took the sins of the whole world upon him. Say: **If Jesus had simply died, that would make him a nice man. But there's an incredible finish to the story that showed everyone that Jesus was God's Son! Read John 19:38–20:18.** Say: **When Jesus rose from the dead, he conquered death for you and me. If we believe in Jesus, we can have life forever in heaven.**

Show children how to form their nails into a cross. Then distribute six-inch lengths of thin-gauge wire, and help the children wrap their wires around the nails where they intersect. Pass out twelve-inch lengths of leather lacing. Have the children slip the laces through the wires and then tie the ends of the laces together to make necklaces.

Kids can wear their cross necklaces as a reminder of the pain Jesus went through to give us new life.

JOHN
20:24-29

THEME:
We can believe in Jesus.

SUMMARY:
Use this SKIT to show children the amazing things Jesus did while he was on earth.

THE AMAZING, ALMIGHTY, UNBELIEVABLE JESUS!

SCENE: Four of Jesus' disciples and Mary are gathered in a room.

PROPS: You'll need tables, chairs, cups, and a large box fan.

CHARACTERS:
Thomas (disciple dressed in "biblical" clothing; bathrobes work well)
Mary (dressed in "biblical" clothing)
James (disciple dressed in "biblical" clothing)
Peter (disciple dressed in "biblical" clothing)
John (disciple dressed in "biblical" clothing)
Narrator

SCRIPT
(The disciples and Mary are sitting or standing around a room, talking with Thomas.)

Thomas: I just don't believe it!

Mary: But Thomas, he was here! Jesus was here!

Thomas: *(Helping Mary to a chair)* Mary, I think you've been working too hard. Why don't you sit down and have something cold to drink?

James: I saw him too, Thomas. Jesus was here!

Thomas: Oh no! Not you too, James! Peter, John, help me out here. These two are scaring me!

Peter: Sorry, Thomas, we all saw him. Jesus came in and showed us the nail marks in his hands and the scar on his side. He said, "Peace be with you." He was as real as you are right now.

John: *(Smiling)* Sure was!

Thomas: *(Shaking head)* But we all saw Jesus die. We saw the soldiers nail him to the cross. Heard his last sigh. We even watched as they laid him in the tomb! *(Pauses.)* Nope, I just can't believe he's alive. Not till I can touch his hands and side, too.

John: Jesus sure had a way of doing some unbelievable things, didn't he? I mean, he was amazing! *(All nod and smile.)*

Peter: *(Excitedly)* Like the time he taught me how to walk on water! I can still feel the salty waves tickling my toes.

Mary: Or when he turned water into wine. Boy, were those people surprised!

James: Wait, I've got the best one! When he fed that crowd of five thousand people—with a boy's little lunch! Now that was unbelievable! And it was the best lunch I've ever eaten.

Thomas: Yeah, yeah, OK. I get your point, but those were just…miracles. I mean, how could somebody overcome death? It's just too unbelievable.

James: How is it any different from Jesus raising Lazarus from the dead? *(All nod and agree.)*

John: And all those people he healed—the sick, the blind, the crippled? That seems unreal, but it happened.

Peter: You know Jesus performed those miracles, Thomas. How can you doubt his power now?

Thomas: *(Scratches head, confused.)* I don't know, it's just that… *(shaking head)* …well, it's too impossible. I can't believe he could— *(From offstage, turn a fan on high speed to cause a "wind." All look toward the wind and say, "Jesus!" Turn off the lights.)*

Narrator: Then Jesus said, "You believe because you see me. Those who believe without seeing me will be truly happy."

If you use this skit as a discussion starter, here are possible questions:

■ **How do we doubt Jesus' power today?**

■ **Why is it so important that we believe in Jesus?**

■ **What helps you believe in Jesus even when you can't see him?**

■ **Why do you think Jesus performed so many miracles when he was on earth?**

■ **What miracles do you see today?**

JOHN 21:4-17

THEME:

Jesus forgives our sins.

SUMMARY:

Use this CREATIVE STORY-TELLING activity to teach children that Jesus forgave Peter and that Jesus forgives us, too.

PREPARATION: You'll need a Bible.

FISH AND FORGIVENESS

Open your Bible to John 21:4-17 to show children where the passage comes from. Say: **This Bible story is about a time Jesus appeared to his friends after he rose from the dead. Listen for the special question that Jesus asks Peter.** Have the children join you in doing the italicized motions throughout the story.

After Jesus died and rose again, he appeared to his disciples many times. Each time they saw Jesus, the disciples were amazed that he'd actually risen from the dead.

One evening, Peter, Thomas, Nathanael, and some of Jesus' other friends went fishing. They got into a boat and rowed out into the Sea of Galilee. **Let's pretend we're in the boat with Jesus' friends.** *(Form pairs, and have partners sit facing each other so the bottoms of their feet are touching. Then show children how to hold hands and rock back and forth as if they're rowing.)*

After the men found a good fishing spot, they cast their nets into the water, hoping to catch lots of tasty fish. *(Pretend to toss a large net into the water.)* When the men pulled the nets in *(pretend to pull in a net)*, there wasn't a single fish! All night they tossed their nets into the water *(continue to cast and then pull in a net)*, but they didn't catch anything.

Just as dawn was casting its yellow light over the water, the disciples heard a voice calling them from the shore.

"Friends," the man called, "haven't you caught any fish?"

The men shook their heads. "No," they replied, "not even one!"

Then the man on the shore called to them, "Throw your net out from the right side of the boat, and you'll find some fish."

The men sighed. It had been a long night, and they were tired. *(Yawn and stretch.)* Did this stranger really think they'd catch anything now? But it couldn't hurt, so the disciples tossed their net once more—this time on the right side of the boat. *(Pretend to toss a net to your right.)*

Suddenly, the net became so heavy that it was about to break! All the disciples had to help to try to pull in the net! *(Pretend to pull in the heavy net.)* The net was so full of fish that the men couldn't even pull it into the boat! They dragged it behind them as they rowed back to shore. *(Pretend to row again with your partner.)* When the disciples got to the shore, they discovered that the stranger who had talked to them was Jesus!

They all gathered for a fish breakfast there on the sandy beach. After they ate, Jesus asked Peter, "Do you truly love me more than anything?"

"Yes, Lord," Peter said. "You know I love you."

Then Jesus asked again, "Do you truly love me?"

Again Peter answered, "Yes, Lord. You know that I love you."

A third time, Jesus asked Peter, "Do you love me?"

Peter felt bad that Jesus asked him three times. But Peter remembered that three times, he'd said he didn't know Jesus.

"Lord, you know everything; you know I love you."

Jesus forgave Peter for saying he didn't know him. Jesus wanted Peter to remember how important it is to love him with all your heart.

When we do bad things, Jesus forgives us, too. Let's tell Jesus how much we love him right now.

Close by having children say simple, one-sentence prayers.

ACTS

"But when the Holy Spirit comes to you, you will receive power. You will be my witnesses— in Jerusalem, in all of Judea, in Samaria, and in every part of the world."

Acts 1:8

ACTS 2:1-21

THEME:
God fills us with the Holy Spirit.

SUMMARY:
In this QUIET REFLECTION, children discover that God gives us the Holy Spirit because he loves us.

PREPARATION: You'll need a Bible, paper cups, and a pitcher of water.

Have the children sit in a circle on the floor. Give each child an empty paper cup. Ask:
■ **What's inside your cups?**

Hold up a paper cup, and say: **If we don't have Jesus in our lives, we may be like these cups: empty inside with nothing to give other people.** Pour water into the cup you're holding. Say: **When we believe in Jesus and ask him to be the Lord of our lives, God promises to pour his Spirit into us and fill us with his love, just as the water fills this cup. Let's read what the Bible tells us about God filling us with the Holy Spirit.**

Ask for volunteers to read aloud Acts 2:1-21. If you have young children, read aloud Acts 2:1-4. Then ask:
■ **Why did God give us the Holy Spirit?**
■ **How does God's gift of the Holy Spirit demonstrate his love?**
■ **What happens when we're filled with God's Spirit?** Lead children to mention that God's Spirit

helps us spread God's love to others.

Have children stand in a circle holding their paper cups. Say: **Let's see how being filled with the Holy Spirit helps us pass God's love to others. I'll pour my water into another person's cup as I whisper, "God, thank you for the Holy Spirit." Then that person will pour his or her water into the next person's cup and whisper, "God, thank you for the Holy Spirit." We'll go all the way around the circle.**

Pour your water into the first child's cup, and whisper: **God, thank you for the Holy Spirit.** Have children continue this around the circle until each child has had a turn to fill someone's cup and thank God for his Spirit.

Close with this quiet prayer: **Thank you, God, for giving us your Holy Spirit to strengthen, comfort, and help us understand more about you. We're glad the Holy Spirit helps us pass your love to others. In Jesus' name, amen.**

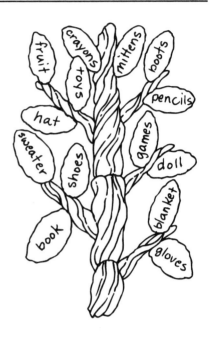

ACTS
3:1-10

THEME:
God wants us to give to people in need.

SUMMARY:
In this SERVICE PROJECT, children give according to what they have.

PREPARATION: You'll need a Bible, brown paper grocery sacks, green construction paper, masking tape, and black markers.

Before class, make a "Giving Tree." Twist brown paper grocery sacks, and then tape the sacks to the wall to create a four-foot-tall tree trunk. Tear pieces from another sack to twist into "branches"; then tape the branches to the trunk. Tear green construction paper into a pile of large leaves.

Set out the paper leaves and black markers. Let children select a service organization to help, such as a children's home, a mission for the homeless, a shelter for abused women and children, or a local food pantry. If you're not sure what agencies are in your area, check the phone book under Social Service Organizations for ideas.

After you've chosen an organization to help, encourage children to think of items they can bring from their homes to donate. For example, a children's home may need toys, clothes, or school supplies. A mission for the homeless may need canned goods, blankets, or warm gloves and hats.

Help children write on the paper leaves the names of the items they thought of. Then have each child tape a leaf or two to the Giving Tree.

Read aloud Acts 3:1-10. Ask:

■ **What did the man at the Beautiful Gate need?**

■ **How did Peter and John help the man?**

Say: **Peter and John didn't have money, but they did have something special to give— Jesus' love! We may not have exactly what someone asks for, but we can give from what we do have, and we always have Jesus' love to give. Our Giving Tree will help us to give others what they need and will help us to spread Jesus' love at the same time.**

You may come to the Giving Tree and pick one or two leaves from the tree. Try to pick leaves with items listed on them that you already have at home to donate. Then bring those items next week.

Help each child pick one or two leaves. If you have nonreaders, read aloud the item listed on each leaf. Be sure children take the leaves home and bring their items in the following week. Then make arrangements to deliver the items. You may wish to visit the organization as a class to allow the children to personally present their items of love.

ACTS 4:32-35

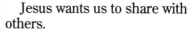

THEME:
Jesus wants us to share with others.

SUMMARY:
Use this SKIT to help children understand the joy that comes from sharing.

GIMME A BREAK!

This skit can be developed into an exciting class project. Encourage everyone to help in one of the following ways: acting out parts, designing program pamphlets, preparing simple sets, or making refreshments to serve after the performance. Invite families, friends, and other classes to enjoy this special play!

SCENE: A family is spending an evening at home.

PROPS: You'll need four chairs, two books, "homework" supplies, a hymnal, a newspaper, a toy cat, a bowl of popped popcorn, and a Bible.

CHARACTERS:
Father Gimme (older boy with a fedora-type hat)
Mother Gimme (older girl wearing a dress and pearls)
Sister Gimme (girl with hair in pigtails)
Brother Gimme (boy wearing baseball cap)
Reader (reads the story from offstage while the Gimmes pantomime their roles)

The Itsmine family (father and mother with three or four children, dressed similarly to the Gimmes)

SCRIPT

(Father Gimme is sitting in a chair reading the newspaper and eating popcorn. Mother Gimme is sitting next to him, petting the cat and eating popcorn from the same bowl. Sister Gimme is sitting on the floor reading a book, and Brother Gimme is lying on the floor doing his homework.)

Reader: Once upon a time, there lived a family named the Gimmes. The Gimmes were an average family for the most part, but there was one problem... *(Mother and Father start fighting over the bowl of popcorn. When Sister turns to watch the popcorn fight, Brother takes her book to use for his homework. She turns around and finds her book gone, then struggles with Brother over the book.)*

Reader: They couldn't share anything! *(Family continues struggling while Reader continues.)* No matter what one family member had, another would soon try to take it away. *(Each family member goes to a different corner and sulks.)*

Reader: It made things very uncomfortable in the Gimme house. *(Each family member takes a chair, then puts the four chairs together to make a car. They sit in the car so their sides are to the audience. Father is driving, and he and Mother fight about which radio station to listen to. Brother and Sister are in the back fighting over a Bible.)*

Reader: Each Sunday, the Gimmes went to church. *(Family members rearrange "car" chairs to form a pew facing the audience. They stand at the pew as if they're singing. Each one tries to pull the hymnal to rest in front of him or her.)*

Reader: They couldn't share the hymnal. *(Family sits down close together, then elbows each other for more space.)*

Reader: They couldn't share the pew. But one Sunday, the pastor said something that made the Gimmes all stop and think for a minute. *(Gimmes stop elbowing and listen.)* He told them about the church in Jerusalem long, long ago. It seems that the believers there shared *everything!* They shared their private property, their money, their houses... everything. And sharing was a good thing! *(The Gimmes look at each other a little embarrassed; then each one moves over to allow more room for the others.)*

Reader: Hmm. Well, if sharing worked for the Christians back then, maybe it would work for the Gimmes right now. They decided to try sharing things for a while. *(Family returns to original setup with Mother and Father sitting and eating popcorn while Brother does homework and Sister reads.)*

Reader: At first, it was hard to share things. *(Mother and Father start to tug back and forth on the bowl of popcorn, then look at each other and smile. Father offers the bowl to Mother.)*

Reader: But soon, it got easier. *(Brother starts to take Sister's book, then stops and asks for the book. Sister smiles, hands the book to Brother, then finds another book nearby.)*

Reader: Eventually, the Gimmes

realized that they actually *liked* sharing! In fact, they *wanted* to share things! *(Brother takes the book back to Sister.)*

Reader: It seemed as if the Gimmes had learned their lesson. And just in time, too, because soon they met their new neighbors... *(After a knocking sound, the Gimmes look up. They go to the "door" together and open it. The Itsmines are standing there, jockeying for position at the door.)*

Reader: The Itsmine family.

Permission to photocopy this skit from *The Children's Worker's Encyclopedia of Bible-Teaching Ideas: NT* granted for local church use. Copyright © Group Publishing, Inc., P.O. Box 481, Loveland, CO 80539.

If you use this skit as a discussion starter, read aloud Acts 4:32-35. Then ask:

■ **How does sharing bring you joy?**
■ **What things are hard for you to share? Why?**
■ **Why does God want us to share what we have with others?**
■ **How do people see God's love when you share?**

ACTS 5:1-11

THEME:
God wants us to be honest.

SUMMARY:
In this LEARNING GAME, children experience sour lies and sweet truths.

PREPARATION: You'll need a Bible and a slice of lemon and large gumdrop for each child.

Gather children and ask:
■ **When have you lied or had someone lie to you?**
■ **Did anyone know you lied? How did you feel?**
■ **What happens when we're not honest?**

Say: **Dishonesty is like a trap. One lie often leads to more, and before you know it, the lies have taken over. God wants us to be honest, and he knows when we're not. Let's read a Bible story about a man and woman who were dishonest before God.**

Have a volunteer read aloud Acts 5:1-11. Then say: **God knows that honesty is important, and he also knows that lies make our hearts sour. Let's play a game called Sour Lies and Sweet Truth. I'll hand each of you a piece of sour lemon and a sweet candy. When I say something untrue, take a lick of lemon. When I say something true, take a lick of sweet candy.** Read the following statements, pausing after each for children to respond.
■ **The sky is purple and green.**
■ **God knows when we're dishonest.**
■ **Two plus four equals twenty.**
■ **Kangaroos live in the ocean.**
■ **God loves us.**
■ **God wants us to be honest.**
Ask:
■ **Why do you think honesty is important to God?**
■ **Does God always know if we're truthful? Explain.**
■ **How can you be truthful in**

all you do and say?

Let children finish their gumdrops. Then end with a prayer, thanking God for his message of honesty.

ACTS
8:1-8

THEME:

God wants us to share our faith during difficult times.

SUMMARY:

Use this CRAFT project to encourage children to share their faith with others even in difficult circumstances.

PREPARATION: You'll need a Bible, tape, dry beans, marbles, and tempera paint. You'll also need shoe-box lids or shallow pans and white construction paper cut to fit inside the lids or pans. Be sure you have a sheet of paper and a box lid or pan for each child.

Hand each child a box lid or pan and a sheet of white paper. Instruct children to place the papers in their containers and then tape them to the edges. Show children how to tape a few beans onto the paper.

Place three or four blobs of paint on each sheet of paper, then hand each child a marble to place in his or her container. Say: **Let's gently rock and roll our marbles and see where the paint trails go.** Encourage children to gently tip their containers back and forth to allow the marbles to roll through the paint and spread it around the papers. You may wish to add different colors of paint to make colorful trails. When children are done, ask:

■ **What kept the marbles from rolling in straight paths?**

■ **How would the paths have been different if the beans hadn't been in the way?**

■ **Did the marbles reach the other side of the containers even though the beans were in the way? Why?**

Say: **Sometimes things stand in our way of telling others about Jesus. We might be afraid to tell others or may worry about what people will think. But it's important to know we can tell others the good news even when times are tough. Let's read about the first Christians and how they told others about Jesus even when the going was rough.**

Have a volunteer read aloud Acts 8:1-8. Then ask:

■ **Why do you think people like Philip kept telling others about Jesus?**

■ **What might have happened if Christians like Philip had stopped telling others about Jesus?**

Hold up a lid, and say: **Just as there were obstacles in your containers, sometimes there are obstacles in our lives. Maybe we didn't get the part in the school play or we lost something special or got sick the day of our best friend's party. We need to remember that when times are tough, we can still spread the good news about Jesus just as the marbles spread the paint in our containers. When we tell** others about Jesus even when times are tough, we paint a beautiful picture of love! Hold up a painted paper.

Have children make cards by folding their decorated papers. Encourage children to write brief notes inside the cards telling about Jesus. Nonreaders can draw pictures of Jesus.

ACTS 9:1-19

THEME:
God reveals himself to Saul on the road to Damascus.

SUMMARY:
In this CREATIVE STORYTELLING activity, children take an imaginary journey to the city of Damascus.

PREPARATION: You'll need a Bible.

SAUL MEETS JESUS

Open your Bible to Acts 9:1-19 to show children the passage. Then read the following story, encouraging children to join you in doing the motions.

Hi! *(Wave hello.)* **My name is Saul. I want to tell you an exciting story about a trip I took to the city of Damascus. Wow, was it exciting! I found out that Jesus had a special plan for my life. It happened like this...**

A long time ago, I was mean and nasty. Grrr! *(Shake your fists and make growling sounds.)* **I didn't**

like Christians, and I wanted all of 'em in jail!** *(Put hands in front of your eyes with your fingers spread like jail bars.)* **I didn't believe in this Jesus guy** *(shake your head)*, **and I didn't want others to follow him. So I got permission from the high priest to arrest all the Christians I could find in Damascus. I was going to bring them back to Jerusalem as my prisoners.** *(Cross your wrists in front of you as if in handcuffs or chains.)*

My friends and I set off for our journey to Damascus. *(Walk in place.)* **All of a sudden, I saw a brilliant light from heaven flash all around me.** *(Shield your eyes with your hands.)* **The light was so blinding that I fell to the ground.** *(Fall to the floor.)* **Ahh! Then I heard a voice say, "Saul, Saul, why are you persecuting me?"**

I couldn't see anything, so I asked, "Who's talking to me?" *(Shield your eyes and shake your head.)*

The voice said, "I am Jesus, whom you are persecuting. Get up and go into the city. Someone there will tell you what you must do."

Whoa! I was shocked! *(Jump to your feet and stare in disbelief.)* **I mean, this was Jesus talking to me!** *(Point to yourself.)* **My friends stood there speechless. They heard his voice, too, but they couldn't see anyone. Then I realized I was blind.** *(Close your eyes and wave your arms in front of you.)* **My friends took my hand and led me into the town of Damascus.** *(Join hands with a* *friend and walk in place.)* **I was blind for three days and didn't eat or drink anything.**

In the city of Damascus, there was a man who loved Jesus. *(Put your hand over your heart.)* **His name was Ananias** (An-uh-NY-us)**. The Lord spoke to Ananias in a dream and told him to find me and lay his hands on me so I could see again. But Ananias was afraid.** *(Tremble as if you're afraid.)* **He knew I had come to arrest Christians, and he was a Christian and didn't want to go to jail.** *(Put your hands in front of your eyes with your fingers spread like jail bars.)*

But the Lord told Ananias, "Go! *(Point with authority.)* **I have chosen Saul for an important work. He must tell many people about me."** *(Spread your arms wide.)* **Even though Ananias didn't understand, he had faith in the Lord. So Ananias found me, then placed his hands on me.** *(Put your hands on a friend's shoulders.)* **He said, "Jesus sent me so that you could see again and be filled with the Holy Spirit."**

Wow! Guess what happened then? Something like fish scales fell from my eyes, and I could see again! I wasn't blind any longer! *(Cover your eyes, then uncover them and open them wide.)* **After that, I believed in Jesus and came to love him.** *(Kneel as if in prayer.)* **And I wasn't mean to the Christians any longer. Do you know why? Because I was a Christian too! Yea!** *(Clap and cheer.)*

ACTS 12:1-18

THEME:
Praying with other believers is powerful.

SUMMARY:
Use this creative PRAYER to encourage children to pray with each other.

PREPARATION: You'll need a Bible and a sturdy blanket.

Spread the blanket on the floor. Have children stand around the edges of the blanket without touching it. Have an adult or large child lie on the blanket, then say: **Let's see if one of you can carry the person on the blanket.** Let one or two children try to lift the blanket and carry the person. Then say: **Carrying someone on a blanket isn't easy to do by yourself. But what happens when lots of people join in? Let's see!** Encourage everyone to hold an edge of the blanket, gently lift the person, and carry him or her a few feet across the room. Say: **See? When we all join together, we're stronger!** Gently set the blanket and the person down.

Say: **When we work together, great things happen. Prayer is just like that. When lots of people pray together, wonderful things happen. Let's read a story about a time lots of people joined in prayer.**

Read aloud Acts 12:1-18, then reread verses 5 and 12 aloud. Ask:

■ **What happened when the people prayed for Peter?**

■ **Why is it important to pray for others? with others?**

Say: **Praying with other people is powerful. It shows God that we agree on what we want. God knows we're really serious about our prayers. Let's form groups of three and pray together to thank God for people to pray with.** Help children form groups of three. Then pray: **Dear God, thank you for giving us the gift of prayer. Please help us remember to pray with others and to pray for other people. We're glad you hear every prayer. Thank you, God. In Jesus' name we pray, amen.**

ACTS
14:8-18

THEME:
Only God is worthy of praise and worship.

SUMMARY:
In this LEARNING GAME, children learn that it's important to worship God and give him praise.

PREPARATION: You'll need a Bible and pencils. You'll also need photocopies of the "Who's Worthy?" list (page 104). You'll need one list for every three children.

Have children form groups of three. Instruct each group to choose a Reader, a Recorder, and a Reporter. Then hand the Reader in each group a photocopied list and the Recorder in each group a pencil.

Say: **We're going on a hunt for someone special, and your job is to find that someone. Have the Readers in your groups read aloud the descriptions on the lists. Discuss who might fit that description; then have the Recorder write that person's name beside the description. When we're finished, we'll have the Reporters read the names you've written down.**

Give children five minutes to read and discuss the descriptions. Then call time, and have the Reporters read the names they've written down. Ask:

■ **Can a human being fit these descriptions? Why not?**

■ **How does it feel to know that only God can do all these things?**

■ **Why do you think God is the only one worthy of our praise and worship?**

Read aloud Acts 14:8-18. Then ask:

■ **Is God the only one who can do all these things?**

■ **In what ways can we worship God?** Lead children in naming ways such as reading the Bible, learning about God, praying, and helping others.

Say: **God is mightier than anything or anyone and is the only one worthy of worship and praise. Let's close with a prayer thanking God for who he is.** Pray: **Dear God, we thank you for being all that you are. You are more powerful than anything and stronger than anyone. We give you thanks for your wondrous acts and for your love. In Jesus' name, amen.**

Who's Worthy?

1. **Created the world**
2. **Makes plants grow**
3. **Heals people**
4. **Provides food for all creatures**
5. **Performs miracles**
6. **Made the sky**
7. **Loves us all the time**
8. **Lives in heaven**
9. **Gives mercy and grace**
10. **Is more powerful than anything or anyone**
11. **Made the sea**
12. **Gave us his Son**
13. **Created people**

ACTS
16:16-34

THEME:
We can praise God all the time.

SUMMARY:
Use this MUSIC IDEA to teach children that there's always a way to praise God, no matter what the circumstances are.

PREPARATION: You'll need a Bible. You may also want to use a cassette tape of a familiar song such as "This Is the Day," "Lord, I Lift Your Name on High," or "Jesus Loves Me."

Pick a familiar praise song; then have the children sing it through at least one time. Encourage children to clap and move to the music.

Divide the children into five groups:
■ the No-Eyes *(cover eyes with hands)*
■ the No-Ears *(plug ears with fingers)*
■ the No-Voice *(cover mouths with hands)*
■ the No-Hands *(hold hands behind backs)*
■ the No-Feet *(sit on the floor cross-legged)*

Say: **Let's sing our praise song again and see if we can praise God in different ways. If you're a member of the No-Eyes group, you'll have to praise God with your eyes closed. If you're in the No-Ears group, you'll have to praise God with your ears plugged. If you're in the No-Voice group, you may clap or** sing or move around, but you can't use voices. **If you're in the No-Hands group, you may stomp or sway or sing, but you can't use your hands. If you're in the No-Feet group, you may not walk or hop to praise God, but you can clap or sway back and forth. Ready? Let's praise God!**

Sing or play the song once more. When the song is done, ask:
■ **Was it difficult for anyone to sing or praise God? Explain.**
■ **How did you express your praise to God?**
■ **Did you all find a way to praise God?**

Read aloud Acts 16:16-34. Then say: **Sometimes we feel like Paul and Silas felt—tied up in difficult circumstances. But just as Paul and Silas found a way to praise God, we each found a way to praise God by singing or moving in rhythm to the music. We can find ways and reasons to praise God no matter what we're going through and no matter where we are. We can praise God all the time.** Have children form new groups and sing the praise song again.

ACTS
27:9-39

THEME:
God wants us to make wise choices.

SUMMARY:
Use this active DEVOTION to challenge older children to make wise choices for God.

PREPARATION: You'll need a Bible.

EXPERIENCE

Have each child find a partner. If you have more than twelve children, form small groups of three or four. Say: **Every day we have choices to make. Some, like deciding what to wear or what to eat for lunch, are fairly easy. But many decisions are tough—whether to be friends with someone or whether to obey parents, for example. We want to be sure we're making wise decisions that God approves of. Let's act out some situations where tough decisions have to be made. See if you can decide with your partners what God would have you do. Then we'll discuss your opinions.**

Read the following scenarios; then have each pair of children act out the situation. Read aloud the question following each scenario, and allow a few minutes of discussion to decide on the best solution.

Scenario 1: **You're at a friend's house, and he wants you to watch a movie that your parents told you not to watch. What do you choose to do?**

Scenario 2: **You're at school and notice that your best friend is cheating on a test. What do you choose to do?**

Scenario 3: **You're walking to school and notice that your elderly neighbor's dog is loose. If you help, you might be late for school. What do you choose to do?**

Scenario 4: **You find a fifty-dollar bill on the floor at the grocery store. What do you choose to do? What do you do if it's a one-dollar bill?**

Scenario 5: **You get your math test back and notice that the teacher forgot to mark three answers wrong. If you tell her, your grade will drop. What do you choose to do?**

Scenario 6: **You told your friend you'd sit with her on the field trip. Now you want to sit with someone else even though you know it will hurt your friend's feelings. What do you choose to do?**

RESPONSE

After all the scenarios have been acted out, have children gather together as a group. Then ask:

■ **Would God think you made wise decisions? Why or why not?**

■ **Why is it important to make choices God approves of?**

Ask volunteers to read aloud Acts 27:9-39. Ask:

■ **The men on the ship were faced with a tough decision. Did they make the right choice? Explain.**

■ **What should the sailors have done when Paul warned them about sailing? Why?**

■ **What can you do when you're faced with a tough decision?**

CLOSING

Say: **Choices are sometimes hard, but if we seek God's help, we'll make the right decisions. Let's pray and ask God to help us make wise choices.** Pray: **Dear God, we're glad that we don't have to make difficult decisions on our own, and we thank you for your help. Let us remember to pray and ask for your guidance and help. Thank you, Lord, that you'll show us what to do just as you showed Paul. In Jesus' name, amen.**

ROMANS

"When people sin, they earn what sin pays—
death. But God gives us a free gift—life
forever in Christ Jesus our Lord."

Romans 6:23

ROMANS 3:10, 23-24

THEME:
Everyone needs Christ's love and forgiveness.

SUMMARY:
In this OBJECT LESSON, children examine popcorn to discover that everyone needs forgiveness.

PREPARATION: You'll need a Bible, popped popcorn, napkins, and paper lunch sacks.

Before class, prepare one bag of popcorn for every six children.

Hand each child a napkin. Tell children to form six groups; then place a bag of popcorn in the center of each group. Say: **Let's pretend we're popcorn inspectors in search of the "perfect" kernel of popcorn. Your job is to examine kernels of popcorn and find one you think is perfect, unbroken, and without spots.**

Let the children have a few minutes to look through their popcorn. Then ask:

■ **Did anyone find a "perfect" kernel of popcorn? If you did, hold it up.** Look at all the kernels, and point out that although they may look spotless, they all have spots—in the center of the kernels. Ask:

■ **Are any kernels of popcorn truly perfect? Explain.**

■ **How are kernels of popcorn like people? Are there any perfect people?**

Have a volunteer read Romans 3:10, 23-24. Say: **In some ways, people are like popcorn. We're not perfect, and we all have little spots. We call these spots "sins." Sins are things we've said and done that God tells us are wrong.** Ask:

■ **Who's the only one who can forgive our sins?**

Say: **Because of Jesus, God will forgive our sins so we can be close to God and live with him forever. Let's thank God for sending his Son, Jesus, to die on the cross so we could be forgiven.** Pray: **Dear God, thank you for loving us enough to send your Son, Jesus, to die for our sins. We thank you for forgiving us and for allowing us to be your friends again. In Jesus' name, amen.**

Serve fresh popcorn to enjoy.

ROMANS
5:6-8

THEME:
Jesus died for us because he loves us.

SUMMARY:
Use this creative PRAYER to help children discover how much Jesus loves us.

PREPARATION: You'll need a Bible and a bowl of Hershey's Kisses and Hugs candies.

Have the children sit in a circle. Place the bowl of Kisses and Hugs in the center of the circle.

Ask:

■ **What does it mean when someone loves us?**

■ **What are ways people show their love?** Lead children to mention ways such as being kind, giving hugs, helping each other, and giving special gifts.

Say: **Love is a special gift we give to people. And we all show love in different ways. Some people give hugs to demonstrate their love. Other people draw pictures. And some people may sing beautiful songs to express their love. We know that God loves us, but do you know the very, very special way God showed his love for us? Let's read from the Bible to find out. When you hear how God showed his love, put your hand over your heart.**

Read aloud Romans 5:6-8. Then ask:

■ **How did God show his love for us?** Help the children understand that God showed his love by sending his Son, Jesus, to die for our sins.

■ **Why was this the best gift of love the world has known?**

Say: **God loves us so much that he sent his only Son to die for us. And God sent Jesus not because we're good or deserved him, but because God loves us. God went way beyond hugs and kisses to show his love—he sent Jesus!**

Let's pass the bowl of candy Hugs and Kisses. Take one of each, but don't eat them yet. When everyone has two candies, we'll say a prayer thanking God for his wondrous love.

Pass the bowl of candies around the circle. When everyone has a candy hug and kiss, say: **Let's say a** special prayer before we enjoy our special candies. Pray: **Dear God, we know that love is shown in many ways—through kisses, through helping others, through being kind, and even through our prayers. Lord, there are many ways you have shown us your love, but the best way was by sending your only Son, Jesus, to die for our sins. We thank you, God, for your great love, which is better than chocolate, better than kisses, better than hugs, better than anything in the world! We love you, God. Amen.**

ROMANS 6:23

THEME:
God gives us eternal life through Jesus Christ.

SUMMARY:
Use this SERVICE PROJECT to help children spread the news of God's gift of eternal life.

PREPARATION: You'll need a Bible, colored markers, scissors, ribbon, and a hole punch. You'll also need a roll of Life Savers candy for each child and photocopies of the life preserver ring below.

Before class, photocopy the life preserver ring on stiff paper; then

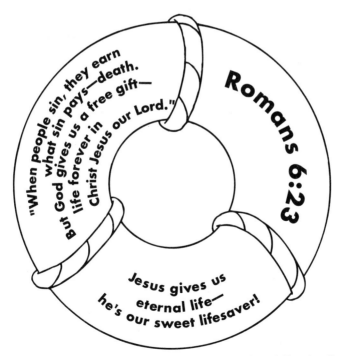

cut out the rings. Be sure to pre-pare a ring for each child.

Set out the paper rings, markers, scissors, ribbon, and rolls of Life Savers candy. Gather children and ask:

■ **What's a life preserver ring used for on a boat?**

■ **What might happen if you don't have a life preserver ring when you need one?**

Say: **Life preservers can save our lives if we're drowning. Did you know that Jesus is like a life preserver? Let's find out how Jesus can save our lives when we're drowning in troubles.**

Have a volunteer read Romans 6:23 aloud. Ask:

■ **What do people earn when they sin?**

■ **What was the free gift God gave us?**

■ **Who gives us eternal life when we accept him as our life-saver?**

Say: **Jesus is our life preserv-er because he saved our lives from sin and death. Without Jesus in our lives, we have sin. And when we have sin, we have death. But God gave us a free gift. He sent Jesus to die for our sins and bring us eternal life.**

Hold up one roll of Life Savers, and say: **Jesus is our lifesaver. And his love is free for everyone. We can share this free gift with others who don't know about Jesus. Let's make special cards to tell others about Jesus, our lifesaver.**

Have each child decorate a paper life preserver using markers. Help each child cut an eight-inch length of ribbon. Then show children how to punch a hole in the paper ring and tie the ribbon through the hole. Tie a roll of Life Savers candy to the other end of each ribbon.

Encourage children to pass out the cards to friends or family mem-bers who don't know about God's free gift of eternal life. Remind them to tell others about Jesus and how he is our life preserver.

ROMANS
8:37-39

THEME:
Nothing can take away God's love.

SUMMARY:
Use this SKIT to help children understand that God's love is more powerful than anything.

DR. LUNEY'S (NOT SO) AMAZING DISCOVERY

SCENE: Outside

PROPS: You'll need a white lab coat, a spray bottle of water, a bas-ketball, baggy pants, silly boxer shorts, a book, and a four-sided box with its flaps cut off (see page 111). You may need to prop the box up with something small, such as a small stone, on one side; just be sure that Dr. Luney is able to subtly knock down the box on cue.

CHARACTERS:
Dr. Luney (a mad scientist—preferably an older child)
Boy (any age, wearing baggy pants

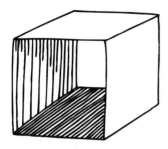

with boxer shorts underneath)
Girl (any age)
Jill (an "audience" member—before the skit, plant Jill in the front row of the audience)

SCRIPT

(Dr. Luney enters, laughing hysterically. He's wearing a lab coat, has his hair teased up and out, and is carrying a spray bottle of liquid.)

Luney: *(Laughing)* Aha! I've finally done it! *(Holds spray bottle up to audience.)* This little bottle will make me famous and rich, rich, *rich!* What is it, you ask? Come closer and I'll tell you. *(Moves closer to the audience and whispers loudly)* It dissolves *everything!* *(Laughs hysterically.)* *Everything!* What? You don't believe me? Well, I'll just show you how well it works. *(Looks around for his first "victim.")*

(Boy enters, dribbling a basketball.)

Luney: Young man, I need to conduct an experiment. Would you kindly step behind this tree for a moment?

Boy: Sure, I guess.

(Boy steps offstage and quickly drops baggy pants while Luney sprays the liquid so audience can see it.)

Boy: *(From offstage)* Hey, wait a minute! You're getting me wet! And you're—hey, hey, you! *(Runs across stage, wearing the silly boxer shorts.)* What'd you do with my pants? I'll get you for this! *(Runs offstage.)*

Luney: *(Laughing)* You see, it does work. But maybe you still don't believe me.

(Girl enters, reading book.)

Luney: Watch!

(Girl moves to the box and stands in front of it as if she's going to sit down. Luney sprays the box, then discreetly steps on the bottom edge to make it collapse. Girl tries to sit down but falls to floor.)

Girl: Hey, what—there was a bench here, wasn't there? It's like it disappeared or something! *(Exits, scratching head.)*

Luney: You see? *(Yelling)* It works! This solution dissolves everything! I'm going to be rich and famous! I love that—especially the rich part!

Jill: *(Stands up from the audience.)* I know something your silly solution can't dissolve.

Luney: What? Who are you? What are you talking about? Of course it can dissolve everything.

Jill: *(Stepping to the stage)* I'm Jill, and I know something it can't dissolve—God's love.

Luney: God's love? *(Baffled)* But... of course it can. You see, I'll just spray all around you. *(Sprays around Jill.)* There. God's love will disappear.

Jill: *(Laughs.)* Wrong! You can't make God's love disappear, Dr. Luney. The Bible says that *nothing*—and that means nothing—can separate us from the love of God. Not even your silly solution.

Luney: *(Puts hands on head.)* Aargh! No, it can't be! My solution is perfect and can dissolve anything! Here, let me try again. *(Holds bottle up to spray Jill, but Jill grabs the bottle from him.)*

Jill: No, let me try again. Maybe your solution is good for something after all. *(Chases Luney offstage, spraying him.)*

If you use this skit as a discussion starter, read aloud Romans 8:37-39. Ask:

■ **How does God show his powerful love for us?**

■ **How do we try to move away from God's love?**

■ **What does it mean to you to know that nothing can keep you from God's love?**

ROMANS 10:10-13

THEME:
We can trust Jesus.

SUMMARY:
Use this QUIET REFLECTION to teach children they can trust Jesus in every area of their lives.

PREPARATION: You'll need a Bible, pens, a hole punch, one-fourth-inch-wide ribbon, scissors, and colored poster board.

Before this activity, cut a twenty-four-inch length of ribbon for each child. You'll also need to cut two poster board keys for each child

using the patterns above. Punch out the holes in the keys using a hole punch.

Gather the children together, and ask:

■ **What does it mean to trust someone?**

■ **Who is someone you trust all the time?**

■ **Can we trust God to help us and always love us? Explain.**

Have a volunteer read aloud Romans 10:10-13. Ask:

■ **In what ways can you trust Jesus to care for you?**

■ **Will everyone who trusts in Jesus have eternal life? How do you know?**

Have children form pairs or trios, and give each child two poster board keys and a piece of ribbon. Say: **We often have troubles and worries that get us down or make us afraid. But we know that Jesus has the key to helping us. Jesus loves us and will help us when we trust him. Think of a worry or fear you have today. It might have to do with your family or school or friends. Draw pictures of or write about those worries or fears on your keys. Then string your keys on the ribbon and tie the ends to make a "key chain" necklace.**

Help children with their keys and ribbons. Then gather the children for a closing prayer. Pray: **Dear God, we're glad we can trust Jesus in every part of our lives. We're happy that there is nothing too big for Jesus to handle and that he has the key to helping us with worries and fears. To show you how much we trust Jesus, we give him the key to our lives. In Jesus' name we pray, amen.**

Say: **Wear your key chains home to remind you that we can always trust in Jesus.**

ROMANS
12:1-2

THEME:
God wants us to give our lives to him.

SUMMARY:
In this OBJECT LESSON, children learn they can give themselves to God as a gift of love.

PREPARATION: You'll need a Bible, small boxes, white tissue paper, bows, colored markers, tape, and scissors.

Before class, wrap a small gift box, and put a bow on top of the package.

Hold up the wrapped gift box to show the children. Ask:
∎ **What does it mean when you give someone a gift?**
∎ **When have you given some-** one a special gift? How did that person feel?

Say: **Giving gifts is a nice way to say, "I love you." God gives us many wonderful gifts because he loves us, but did you know that God would like a special gift from us, too? Let's read from the Bible to find out what we can give God.**

Read aloud Romans 12:1-2. Ask:
∎ **What does God want us to do with our lives?**
∎ **What's a special gift we can give to God?**

Say: **Giving God the gift of ourselves is the best present we can give him. Some of the ways we can give to God are through kindness to others, by helping others, and by praying. Let's pretend that we're wrapping ourselves up as special gifts to God.**

Set out the tissue paper, tape, scissors, colored markers, and bows. Hand each child a small box to wrap and then decorate with markers. Tell children to add colorful bows to their packages. Encourage children to take their "presents" home to remind them to give themselves to God every day.

ROMANS
13:1-7

THEME:
God gives us rules to live by.

SUMMARY:
Use this PARTY to show children that obeying God's rules can be fun.

PREPARATION: You'll need a Bible, construction paper, scissors, tape, crepe paper, markers, glue sticks, and party snacks.

As children arrive at the party, have them make crepe paper seat belts by cutting three-foot lengths of crepe paper and then taping them into loops. Have children wear their seat belts diagonally across their chests during the party.

Decorate the party room with construction paper traffic signs, such as stop signs, yield signs, no U-turn signs, and railroad-crossing signs. Have children obey the signs each time they walk by. Consider letting the children use construction paper, markers, and glue sticks to create their own special "rule" signs. Suggest rules such as "No Messy Rooms Allowed," "Clean Up Your Dishes," or "Danger: Homework Area."

During the party, play games with fun rules, such as Simon Says and Mother May I. Consider serving juice and decorated cookies in the shapes and colors of traffic signs. You may wish to post a list of rules for snack time, such as "Don't chew with your mouth open," "Clean up your area," and "Offer snacks to a friend before serving yourself."

Before the party ends, gather everyone in a group. Say: **We've had fun following party rules.** Ask:

■ **What are rules made for?**

■ **What happens when rules aren't followed?**

Say: **Did you know that God made rules for us to follow, too? Let's see what the Bible says about rules.** Have volunteers read aloud Romans 13:1-7. Say: **Just as there are certain rules that we obey in traffic or in a city, we have rules to obey as Christians. These rules or guidelines are given to us in the Bible.** Ask:

■ **Why do you think God gave us guidelines to live by?**

Say: **God gave us guidelines to live by for our protection and safety. He knows what is best for us. When we obey God, it pleases him. But when we choose to disobey, we pay the consequences for breaking the rules. Let's end our party with a prayer asking God to help us live by his rules.**

Pray: **Dear God, thank you for your rules, which show us your love. We're glad you made rules to protect us and keep us from harm. Please help us obey your rules in everything we say and do. In Jesus' name, amen.**

ROMANS
13:8-12

THEME:
God wants us to love others.

SUMMARY:
In this AFFIRMATION ACTIVITY, children are encouraged to show love to others.

PREPARATION: You'll need a Bible and a flashlight.

Darken the room, and gather children in a circle. Say: **Darkness might remind us of feeling sad or down. There's nothing bright to shine on our hearts and make us happy. But the Bible tells us that love is like a bright light, bringing us joy that we can then shine on others.** Turn on the flashlight, and shine it around the circle. Say: **Let's read what the Bible tells us about love and light.**

Using the flashlight to read by, have volunteers read aloud Romans 13:8-12. Then ask:

■ **Why is it important to love others as you love yourself?**

■ **Can love be a weapon to fight off bad things? How?** Lead children to explain that love battles loneliness, sadness, fear, and hatred.

Say: **The Bible tells us that the world is a dark place, full of bad temptations. When we bring the light of Christ's love to others, it's like shining a light in a dark place.** Shine the flashlight around the room. Say: **The light shining out of a flashlight is like the love in our hearts. We can shine that love on others and take away the darkness they may feel. Jesus wants us to share our love with others. Let's shine a little love on others right now. I'll go first. I'll shine my "love-light" on** (child's name), **and say, "Jesus loves you, and so do I."** Hand the flashlight to the person sitting beside you, and have that person shine his or her lovelight on another child. Continue the affirmations until everyone has had a turn to shine the light and has been in the light.

ROMANS
15:1-8

THEME:
God wants us to encourage others in their faith.

SUMMARY:
Use this creative PRAYER to offer children a chance to encourage their friends.

PREPARATION: You'll need a Bible, a Christmas tree stand, a large tree branch, scissors, tape, markers, and construction paper.

Before class, erect a large tree branch in a Christmas tree stand. The larger the branch, the better. Set out construction paper, markers, and scissors.

Have children get with partners. Ask:

■ **When have you felt dis-**

couraged?

■ What happens when we become too frustrated or discouraged?

Say: We all need encouraging words now and then. Sometimes we have troubles in school, and it helps when a teacher encourages us to do better. Sometimes we have trouble trusting God and need friends to encourage our faith. Let's see what the Bible says about encouraging each other's faith. Have a volunteer read aloud Romans 15:1-8. Ask:

■ What are ways we can encourage each other to grow in our faith?

Say: We can help each other be stronger in our faith by writing each other encouraging notes, by being kind, by praying for one another, and by asking each other how things are going in our relationship with Jesus. Today we're going to encourage our partners' faith. First, you'll need to help your partner make a "prayer leaf." Trace both your hands on construction paper, then cut the tracings out. Glue the paper hands together in "prayer-hands" style, and write your name on one side and your partner's name on the other.

Circulate and offer help as needed. When everyone is finished, say:

Let's stand in a circle and place our paper prayer hands together. We'll say a prayer asking God to encourage the people whose names are written on the paper hands. Then we'll tape the paper hands to our Encouragement Tree as colorful leaves.

Pray: Dear God, thank you for friends who help encourage our faith. Help us see new ways to be encouragers for all the people we know. In Jesus' name, amen.

Have children tape the leaves to the branches as reminders to children that friends encourage one another in their faith.

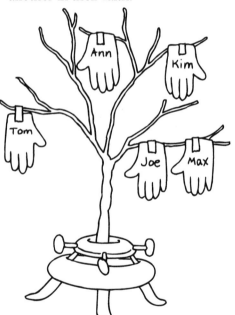

1 CORINTHIANS

*"Don't you know that you are God's temple
and that God's Spirit lives in you?"*

1 Corinthians 3:16

---

1 CORINTHIANS 1:4-9

THEME:
God gives us many blessings.

SUMMARY:
Use this AFFIRMATION ACTIVITY to teach children how God's blessings are all around them.

PREPARATION: You'll need a Bible, balloons, markers, and several one-by-thirteen-inch strips of paper for each child.

Before class, set the markers, paper strips, and balloons out on a table. Do not blow up the balloons yet.

Gather children around you and ask:

∎ **What are special things you know God has given you?** Encourage children to name such things as friends, parents, good food to eat, pretty birds and animals, nice places to live, Jesus, and the Bible.

Say: **God loves us so much that he wants to give us good things. God blesses us in many ways, and his blessings are all around us every day. Let's read about some of the great things God gives us and does for us. Listen carefully to see how many you can remember.** Read aloud 1 Corinthians 1:4-9. Then have children recount God's blessings including God's grace, his riches, gifts, knowledge, and Jesus.

Distribute the slips of paper. Then say: **Let's make "blessing** balloons" to help us remember that God loves us and blesses us in many ways. **Use markers to write or draw pictures of special things God gives us. Then roll the paper strips into tiny rolls, and stuff each one into a balloon. Blow up your balloon, and I'll help you tie it off.**

Circulate to help children as needed. After everyone has blown up a balloon, say: **Let's form a circle, and we'll bop our balloons up and down and back and forth across the circle. We'll mix up the balloons so you won't know where your balloon is. As we bop the balloons, let's say this rhyme: Up to the sky and down to the ground. God's blessings are all around!**

Repeat the rhyme several times as you bop the balloons around the circle. After a few repetitions, tell each child to hold a balloon. Then have children sit on the balloons to pop them and discover the pictures inside. Talk about what each child found and how that picture shows God's blessings.

1 CORINTHIANS
3:4-9

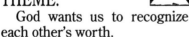

THEME:
God wants us to recognize each other's worth.

SUMMARY:
In this active DEVOTION, children discover that quarreling can spoil things for everyone.

PREPARATION: You'll need a Bible, markers, and tape. You'll also need one two-inch square of paper for each child. You may wish to round the top corners of the paper squares.

EXPERIENCE

Help children form pairs. Say: **We all have had quarrels or arguments before. Tell your partner about a time you argued about something. Be sure to tell how you felt and how you settled your fight. Decide who will talk first; then when I clap, have the other person talk.** Allow a few moments for each partner to talk.

Say: **Quarreling isn't fun, and it makes people feel bad. When Paul wrote to the people in Corinth, he warned them about quarreling. Let's see what Paul said about arguing with other Christians.** Read aloud 1 Corinthians 3:4-9. Ask:

■ **What might happen when we quarrel?**

■ **Is someone more important than someone else? Why or why not?**

■ **How can we treat each other better so there's no arguing or fights?** Lead children to name ways such as helping each other, talking to one another, and being patient and kind with each other.

Say: **Let's make finger puppets to help us learn more about being kind to each other.**

Hand each child a paper square. Invite children to decorate their puppets using markers and then to tape the puppets in tube shapes to fit around their fingers.

When everyone is done, say: **When I say "go," have your puppets argue with each other. Have your puppet say that it's better than your partner's puppet.** Encourage the children to make the arguments lively and realistic.

RESPONSE

After a few moments say: **Stop. Doesn't quarreling sound awful?** Ask:

■ **How did arguing make you feel?**

■ **Can you think of a better way to settle a disagreement rather than quarreling?**

CLOSING

Say: **Put on your finger puppet, and have it touch heads with your partner's finger puppet. Let's pray. Dear God, please help us be kind to one another and see each other's worth instead of quarreling. In Jesus' name we pray, amen.**

1 CORINTHIANS
9:24-27

THEME:
God wants us to learn self-control.

SUMMARY:
In this LEARNING GAME, children realize the importance of self-control.

PREPARATION: You'll need a Bible, masking tape, a ruler, glue,
scissors, and green and red construction paper.

Make a stop-and-go sign by gluing a red construction paper circle to one side of a ruler and a green construction paper circle to the other side.

Young children will especially like this game. With masking tape, mark a starting line at one end of the room. Have the children line up on it. At the opposite end of the room, mark an X on the floor with masking tape. Choose one child to be the Traffic Controller, and hand that child the stop-and-go sign. Have the Traffic Controller stand on the masking tape X.

Say: **Let's play a game called Bumper-to-Bumper. Hold the backs of your knees with your hands, and don't let go. Watch the Traffic Controller to know when to start and stop moving. Try not to bump anyone too hard as you "drive" toward the Traffic Controller. A red light from the Traffic Controller means to stop in place. If the Traffic Controller sees you move during a red light, you'll have to return to the starting line and begin again. A green light from the Traffic Controller means you can drive ahead. You'll have to use lots of self-control to make it to the other side of the room!**

Play the game several times, choosing a new Traffic Controller for each round. Then gather children and read aloud 1 Corinthians 9:24-27. Talk about how racers, even in Paul's time, had to use self-control to win. Explain that racers who go out of control or fail to follow the rules are disqualified.

End by saying: **God wants us to use self-control to follow his rules so we can receive the rewards he has promised us.** For extra fun, have children make edible race cars from graham crackers and icing. Let children attach oyster cracker "wheels" using sticky icing.

1 CORINTHIANS 10:23-29

THEME:

We can stand up for what we believe.

SUMMARY:

Use this MUSIC IDEA to encourage children to be strong in their faith so they can make difficult decisions.

PREPARATION: You'll need a Bible, a marker, and newsprint.

Before class, copy the words to the old, familiar hymn "We'll Stand Up for Jesus" on newsprint for the class to read. You'll find the words to the hymn in the following activity.

Read aloud 1 Corinthians 10:23-29. Then say: **There are always people who are eager to tempt us to do wrong things. It's important that we learn to say "no" to temptation and "yes" to Jesus. When we do what's right—even when others don't like it—it's called standing up for what we believe. And because** we love Jesus and rely on his strength, we can stand up for Jesus whenever someone wants us to do something wrong.

Let's sing a song called "We'll Stand Up for Jesus." Lead children in singing the following song to the tune of "Mary Had a Little Lamb." Do the accompanying motions or encourage children to make up their own creative movements.

We'll stand up for Jesus *(stand and raise arms),* **Jesus, Jesus. We'll stand up for Jesus. We love Jesus so.** *(Wave arms back and forth.)*

We'll run from things we know are wrong *(run in place),* **Know are wrong, know are wrong. We'll run from things we know are wrong. We love Jesus so.** *(Wave arms back and forth.)*

We'll follow in his footsteps *(tiptoe in place),* **Footsteps, footsteps. We'll follow in his footsteps. We love Jesus so.** *(Wave arms back and forth.)*

1 CORINTHIANS 12:12-28

THEME:
God wants us to cooperate with each other.

SUMMARY:
This cooking activity is a great active DEVOTION that helps children discover the importance of cooperation.

PREPARATION: You'll need a Bible, a knife, margarine, raisins, cinnamon-sugar, a tube of frosting, cookie sheets, plastic knives, shortening, paper towels, and access to an oven. You'll also need one loaf of thawed frozen bread dough for every ten children.

Before class, cut each loaf of thawed bread dough into ten equal sections.

EXPERIENCE

Have children wash their hands and then gather at the table. Ask:

■ **When have you worked with someone or helped someone do a job?**

■ **What was helping that person like?**

■ **Why is it a good idea to work with others?**

Say: **Helping and working with others can be lots of fun. And working together gets a lot of work done in a short time. When we work together, it means we're cooperating. Let's cooperate with each other to make a delicious snack.**

Set out plastic knives, bread dough, raisins, cinnamon-sugar, margarine, shortening, paper towels, and cookie sheets. Form four groups: Slicers, Sprinklers, Scoopers, and Setters. The Slicers cut the dough into one-inch-wide slices and then flatten the slices of dough like pancakes. The Sprinklers spread margarine on the flattened dough and then sprinkle raisins and cinnamon-sugar on top. The Scoopers scoop up the edges of the dough and pinch the edges at the tops to seal them. The Setters grease cookie sheets and then set the dough balls on the greased pans with their "seams" down. When the cookie sheets are full, place them in the oven to bake at 375 degrees for about fifteen minutes or until the buns are golden brown.

RESPONSE

While the rolls are baking, read aloud 1 Corinthians 12:12-28. Ask:

■ **What does it mean to cooperate?**

■ **Why do you think God wants us to work together?**

■ **We're told to share each other's happiness and suffering. When have you shared someone's joy or sadness?**

■ **How was making bread a good example of working together as one?**

CLOSING

Let each child "paint" a cross on his or her roll using a tube of frosting. Say a prayer thanking God for others and asking help to cooperate with others.

1 CORINTHIANS
13:4-8a

THEME:
God's love endures forever.

SUMMARY:
Use this DEVOTION to help children remember that God's love lasts forever.

PREPARATION: You'll need a Bible, a table lamp, markers, hair pins, and blue construction paper. You'll need half a sheet of paper and a hair pin for each child.

Before class, remove the rubber ends from the hair pins.

Plug in the lamp, and place it in one corner of the room. Keep the lamp turned off for now. Darken the room slightly. Gather children around the lamp, and place the Bible, markers, hair pins, and sheets of construction paper beside you.

Say: **Sometimes we have problems and worries that might make us feel like we're in the dark. Maybe they even make us feel like no one loves or cares for us. Have you ever felt that way?** Pause for responses, then encourage children to tell about times they've had worries or fears that have made them feel unloved or alone.

Say: **Let's read from the Bible to see what it says about God's love and how love can help us through the worries and problems we have.**

Read aloud 1 Corinthians 13:4-8a. Say: **The apostle Paul wrote this letter to his friends in the city of Corinth. He wanted them to know that God's love is never-ending. In fact, God's love is there for us in good times and bad and whether we're happy or sad.**

Hand each child a sheet of blue construction paper and a hair pin. Challenge children to think of their greatest worries and fears and to "draw" or "write" them on the sheet of construction paper by poking holes through the paper with the hair pins.

After kids have finished with their designs, darken the room, and turn on table lamp. Say: **We can think of God's love as a bright light. His love shines through the darkest problems or fears we have.** Have a child hold his or her paper to the lamp and let the light shine through the holes. Say: **Can you see God's love shining through? That's because God's love is never-ending!**

Let each child have a turn letting "God's love" shine through; then end with a silent prayer of thanks for God's enduring love.

2 CORINTHIANS

"If anyone belongs to Christ, there is a new creation. The old things have gone; everything is made new!"

2 Corinthians 5:17

2 CORINTHIANS
1:3-5

THEME:
God wants us to comfort others.

SUMMARY:
Use this SERVICE PROJECT to develop children's empathy for children in the hospital.

PREPARATION: You'll need a Bible, rolls of tape, yarn, and scissors. You'll also need to collect old wallpaper sample books from home centers or interior decorating stores. Most stores will give you old sample books for free—especially if you tell them it's for a church or community project. You'll also need photocopies of the directions on page 124 for making wallpaper "beads." You'll need one copy for each wallpaper book you've collected.

Set out tape, yarn, scissors, and the wallpaper books. Ask children if they've ever felt very sick or had to stay in bed for long periods of time. Talk about how it must feel to stay in the hospital for weeks. Then read aloud 2 Corinthians 1:3-5. Say: **It's no fun when someone is hurting or sick. God wants us to help people who need comforting, and today we're going to help children who are in the hospital be a little happier. We'll send them Beautiful Bead kits so they can make pretty friendship bracelets, necklaces, and other crafts.**

Step 1:

Cut a 2-inch square of wallpaper.

Step 2:

Tightly roll from one corner to the other.

Step 3:

Tape the roll so it won't unroll.

Step 4:

String the bead on yarn.

Permission to photocopy these instructions from *The Children's Worker's Encyclopedia of Bible-Teaching Ideas: NT* granted for local church use. Copyright © Group Publishing, Inc., P.O. Box 481, Loveland, CO 80539.

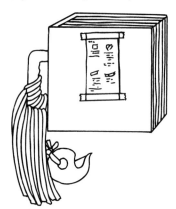

Show children how to assemble the kits by first taping a photocopy of the bead directions to the cover of each wallpaper book. Then cut several twenty-inch lengths of yarn for "patterns," and have children cut at least twenty pieces of yarn for each wallpaper book. Tie the strands of yarn to the handle of each book so children in the hospital will have ready-made loops for stringing their wallpaper beads.

Next, tie a plastic tape dispenser to one of the strands of yarn on each book.

After the kits are done, encourage children to make wallpaper bead friendship necklaces or bracelets to remind them that God wants us to comfort others who are sick or hurting. Arrange for the children to deliver the kits to a local children's hospital or hospital unit.

2 CORINTHIANS 2:5-11

THEME:
God wants us to forgive others.

SUMMARY:
During this PRAYER activity, children are encouraged to focus on forgiving someone who has hurt them.

PREPARATION: You'll need a Bible and a paddle ball toy found in most toy stores (a paddle to which a small rubber ball is attached with an elastic string).

Have children sit in a large circle. Stand and hit the paddle ball several times. Point out how the ball always comes back. As you continue to hit the ball, say: **After we do or say something hurtful, we wish we could pull back our words or actions just as the elastic string pulls back this ball.** Stop batting the ball and ask:
■ **When has someone said or done something that made you**

feel bad?

■ Did you forgive that person? Why or why not?

■ What do you think God wants us to do when someone is rude or hurtful to us?

Say: **Let's read from 2 Corinthians in the Bible. When you know what God wants us to do, put your hand over your heart.** Read aloud 2 Corinthians 2:5-11. Then say: **I see your hands covering your hearts. What does God want us to do?** Pause for children's responses. Then say: **Let's read verse 7 again. "But now you should forgive him and comfort him to keep him from having too much sadness and giving up completely." It's important to forgive others even when they've made us feel bad. And God promises that when we forgive others, forgiveness will come back to us—just like this ball!** Paddle the ball one more time.

Say: **Let's stand and say a prayer in a different way today. I'll begin the prayer and will then leave a blank place for you to silently fill in someone's name who needs your forgiveness. I'll pass the paddle ball around the circle. When it's your turn, give the ball a gentle bop and think of that person's name. Ready?**

Pray: **Dear God, we know that sometimes people say or do things that hurt us. And we know you want us to forgive them. God, please help me forgive** (pass the paddle ball around the circle, and have each child think of someone they'd like to forgive). **We're so glad you forgive and love us. In Jesus' name, amen.** Pass the ball once more around the circle, and encourage children to say "amen."

2 CORINTHIANS 4:13-18

THEME:
We can have faith even when we can't see things.

SUMMARY:
This edible OBJECT LESSON helps children realize that faith is the assurance of things unseen.

PREPARATION: You'll need a Bible, margarine, an electric skillet, a spatula, paper plates, napkins, plastic forks, and a raw egg for each child. You may wish to have fresh fruit on hand for any children who are unable to eat eggs.

Hold up a raw egg. Ask:

■ **What's inside this egg?**

■ **How do you know what's inside when you can't see inside?**

■ **Do we need to see things with our eyes to know something is real? Explain.**

Say: **God wants us to know that we don't need to see everything to know it's real. We can't see the wind, but we see what it does, so we know the wind is real. We can't see God's love, but we see what his love does, so we know God is real. Know-**

ing things without having to see them is called faith. Let's read about having faith from 2 Corinthians 4:13-18.

Read aloud 2 Corinthians 4:13-18. Then hold up the raw egg and ask:

■ **How is having faith like knowing what's in this egg?**

Say: **It's important to have strong faith and know that faith is real. Let's make some "faith eggs" right now to see if your faith was right when it told you there were yolks and whites in these eggs.**

Hand each child an egg, and help him or her crack the egg into the electric skillet. Cook the eggs over medium heat until they're scrambled and done. If you have older children, let them take turns stirring the eggs. Serve the treat on paper plates, and provide napkins and plastic forks.

2 CORINTHIANS 6:3-10

THEME:
God wants us to imitate his love.

SUMMARY:
In this QUIET REFLECTION, children discover that we can spread God's love to others.

PREPARATION: You'll need a Bible and a full-length mirror.

This activity is especially well-suited for young children.

Place a large, full-length mirror at the front of the room, and have children form pairs. Invite each pair to stand in front of the mirror and make motions for the rest of the children to imitate. After everyone has had a turn in front of the mirror, ask:

■ **What does it mean to imitate someone or something?**

■ **How was looking in the mirror an example of imitation?**

■ **Was it easy to imitate everyone's actions? Why or why not?**

Say: **Sometimes it's good to imitate people, especially if they're acting in a good way. God wants us to imitate his love so we can spread it to other people. Let's see what the Bible says about the way we act toward others and how we can imitate God's love.**

Read aloud 2 Corinthians 6:3-10. Then ask:

■ **How can we imitate God's love to others?** Encourage children to name ways such as having patience, serving others, being kind, and speaking the truth.

End the activity by having each child look in the mirror and say, "I can imitate God's love to others."

2 CORINTHIANS 8:8-15

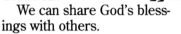

THEME:
We can share God's blessings with others.

SUMMARY:
Use this SERVICE PROJECT to help children realize they can provide for other people's needs.

PREPARATION: You'll need a Bible, a medium-sized box, colorful markers, and photocopies of the parent's letter from page 128.

Select a Native American school or reservation to receive your donations. The week before you plan to use this idea, photocopy the letter from page 128, and have each child take a letter home. This service project is especially effective at the beginning of a school year when school supplies are on sale.

On collection day, gather children in a circle, and let them hold their donations. Place the box and markers in the center of the circle. Say: **I can see you each brought some of your favorite kinds of school supplies. Why do you think it's good to share what you have with people who might not be able to have those things?** Pause for children to give their explanations. Then invite children to show what things they've brought to share. Let the children place the items in the box; then encourage children to decorate the box with the markers.

When the box is finished, gather children in a group to read aloud 2 Corinthians 8:8-15. Point out that God gives us plenty to share with others so no one has too much or too little. End the activity by praying over the box and by asking God to bless the children who will be using the school supplies.

2 CORINTHIANS 11:16-29

THEME:
Being a Christian isn't always easy.

SUMMARY:
In this CREATIVE STORYTELLING activity, children "echo" Paul's trials as he travels to bring Christianity to the world.

PREPARATION: You'll need a Bible.

IT'S NOT EASY

Open your Bible to 2 Corinthians 11:16-29 to show children where the passage comes from. Say: Let's pretend that we're with Paul as he travels to spread the good news about Jesus. You can help tell this story. When I hold up my hand, say, "It's not easy being a Christian, but it's worth it!" Let's say that together. Have children repeat this refrain a few times until they're familiar with the words. Then tell the story below, and encourage children to do the italicized motions in parentheses with you.

Hold up your hand. Say: **It's not easy being a Christian, but it's**

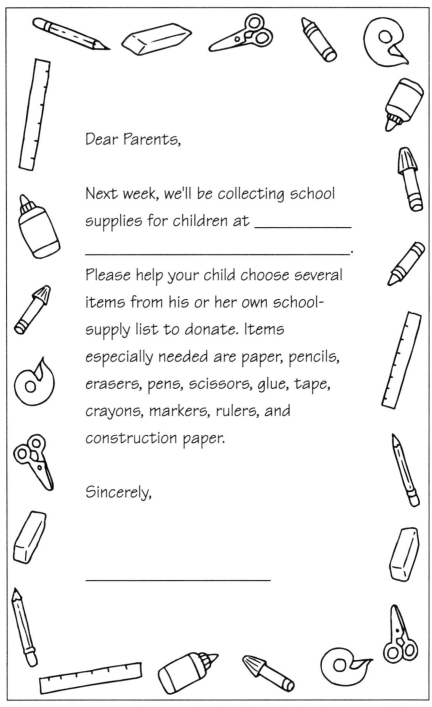

Dear Parents,

Next week, we'll be collecting school supplies for children at _____ _____.

Please help your child choose several items from his or her own school-supply list to donate. Items especially needed are paper, pencils, erasers, pens, scissors, glue, tape, crayons, markers, rulers, and construction paper.

Sincerely,

_____

worth it! I've been in prison many times. *(Hold your hands in front of your face with your fingers spread like prison bars.)* But I never stopped praying or telling others about Jesus. *(Pretend to pray on your knees.)*

Hold up your hand. Say: **It's not easy being a Christian, but it's worth it!** I've been hurt in beatings when people were mean to me because I love Jesus. *(Cringe with arms in front of body as if trying to protect yourself from being beaten.)* But I never stopped telling people that Jesus loves them. *(Point to your heart.)*

Hold up your hand. Say: **It's not easy being a Christian, but it's worth it!** I've been near death many times. I've gone without food *(rub your stomach)* and water *(hold your throat)* and clothing *(shiver)* and even a place to sleep. *(Lie on the floor.)* But I've never stopped loving Jesus or wanting other people to know him.

Hold up your hand. Say: **It's not easy being a Christian, but it's worth it!** Five times I was whipped, and one time people threw large stones at me. *(Pretend to duck flying stones.)* But even through the pain, I never stopped talking about Jesus. *(Point upward.)*

Hold up your hand. Say: **It's not easy being a Christian, but it's worth it!** I've sailed in ships that were wrecked at sea. And once I even had to spend a night and a day in the water, bobbing up and down, afraid I might drown. *(Rock from side to side.)* But I didn't let that stop me from telling people about Jesus or from traveling to set up more churches. *(Make a steeple above your head.)*

Hold up your hand. Say: **It's not easy being a Christian, but it's worth it!** Once when I was in Damascus, the governor wanted to arrest me, so he put guards around the city. *(March like soldiers.)* But I kept praying, and soon my friends lowered me in a basket through a hole in the city wall. I escaped and was free to keep telling others about Jesus. *(Cup your hands around your mouth.)*

Hold up your hand. Say: **It's not easy being a Christian, but it's worth it!** And you can tell others about Jesus, too! *(Point to everyone.)*

GALATIANS

*"But the Spirit produces the fruit of love, joy,
peace, patience, kindness, goodness,
faithfulness, gentleness, self-control. There is
no law that says these things are wrong."*

Galatians 5:22-23

GALATIANS 3:26-29

THEME:
God loves each of us the same.

SUMMARY:
In this OBJECT LESSON, children learn that we're all the same in God's sight.

PREPARATION: You'll need a Bible, paper, and crayons or markers.

Hand each child a sheet of paper and a crayon or marker. Say: **Look around you. There are quite a few people here.** Ask:

■ **How are the people in our room alike? different?**

Say: **We all have similarities and differences. Today you're going to draw pictures of yourselves. But there's one catch—you must draw with the hand you don't normally use. In other words, right-handed people will draw with their left hands, and left-handed people will draw with their right hands. Ready? Draw!**

Allow a few minutes for children to draw with their "difficult" hands. Then call time, and have the children look at the pictures they've drawn. Ask:

■ **Were these pictures difficult to draw? Explain.**

■ **Why do you think some people are right-handed and some are left-handed?**

■ **Does it make a difference to God whether we're right- or** left-handed or whether we're different in other ways? Explain.

Say: **God made us each different. But we're all together in Christ's love. Let's find out what the Bible says about how God loves each of us.**

Read aloud Galatians 3:26-29. Talk about how God loves everyone regardless of race, color, gender, or age. End the activity by singing "Jesus Loves Me." Sing again, but change the words a bit and sing "Jesus Loves You." If time allows, let children finish their pictures.

GALATIANS
4:4-7

THEME:
We are all God's children.

SUMMARY:
Use this CRAFT project to help children understand God's role as a loving, caring parent.

PREPARATION: You'll need a Bible, scissors, tape, crepe paper, and colored ribbon.

If you have young children, you may wish to precut ribbon into eight-inch pieces or tie ribbon bows ahead of time. Prepare five bows or pieces of ribbon for each child.

Begin by reading Galatians 4:4-7 to the children. Focus on verse 7b, which says, "You are God's child, and God will give you the blessing he promised, because you are his child." Ask the children to tell you some of the things their

parents do to care for them, such as provide them with love, food, clothing, and safe places to live.

Say: **Each of us here is part of one big family—God's family. Let's make some "family ties" to remind us that God is our loving Father and that we're his children.**

Help each child cut a two-foot piece of crepe paper. Then have children cut lengths of ribbon and tie colorful bows. Tie the bows down the piece of crepe paper.

After everyone has finished a "family tie," wave the ties and join together for this lively cheer:

I am very glad to be
A part of God's big family!
God's our Fa-ther!

GALATIANS
5:22-23

THEME:
God wants us to be patient, kind, and loving.

SUMMARY:
Use this PARTY idea to celebrate the fruits of the Spirit.

PREPARATION: You'll need a Bible, marker, colorful balloons, and various party supplies described below for the activities you choose.

Decorate the room with colorful balloons to represent fruits. Use long yellow balloons as bananas and round orange and green balloons for oranges and limes. Tie several small purple balloons together for grapes. Write the words "love," "joy," "peace," "patience," "kindness," "goodness," "faithfulness," "gentleness," and "self-control" on the balloons.

Gather children in a group after they arrive for the party. Say: **Have you noticed that we have a lot of "fruity" decorations hanging up? And did you know that God has given us fruits to carry inside us? Let's read about these special fruits God gives us. When I name the fruits, see if you can count them on your fingers.** Read aloud Galatians 5:22-23. Then have children list the fruits of the Spirit. Encourage children to read the balloons if they can't remember all the fruits. After talking about what fruits God has given us and why these are important to have, choose any number of activities below to round out the party.

■ Let children cut up fresh fruit for juicy-good fondue. Combine honey and peanut butter or brown sugar and softened cream cheese for tasty dips.

■ Play a modified version of Fruit-Basket Upset. Have children form groups of three. Two children in each group hold hands to form the Basket. The third child in each group plays the Fruit and must stand in the Basket. Slowly name the fruits of the Spirit. Then call, "Fruit basket upset!" and let the Fruits find new baskets. After a few rounds, have Fruits and Baskets change places.

■ Another fun game is called Fruit Pickin'. Before the party, write the fruits of the Spirit on paper fruits, then hide several sets of the fruits around the room. Have children form pairs, and hand each pair a paper bag. On "go," have children find each of the fruits of the Spirit.

■ For party favors, hand out the fruity balloons used for decorating the room.

While everyone is having fun at the party, affirm children who are exhibiting fruits of the Spirit. For example, you might say, "I notice that Robert is waiting patiently for his turn," and "Sulee didn't get upset when her balloon popped." Ask children to compliment each other when they observe others demonstrating the fruits of the Spirit.

EPHESIANS

"I mean that you have been saved by grace through believing. You did not save yourselves; it was a gift from God."

Ephesians 2:8

EPHESIANS 1:19-23

THEME:
Christ is the foundation of our faith.

SUMMARY:
Use this AFFIRMATION ACTIVITY to help children understand that their faith must be rooted in Jesus.

PREPARATION: You'll need a Bible, tape, scissors, markers, brown poster board, and green construction paper. Cut the poster board into a three-by-seven-inch strip for each child.

Stand like a tree with your arms spread and say: **I'm tall and have leaves and can sway in the breeze. What am I?** When children guess that you're a tree, ask:

■ **What holds a tree in the ground?**

■ **What happens if a plant or tree has no roots?**

Give each child a brown paper strip. Ask children to make their "tree trunks" stand up. After a few failed attempts, say: **These trees need roots to help them stand straight and tall.** Have children make three two-inch cuts on the bases of their paper trunks. Show children how to fold the "roots" of the paper trees alternately back and forth so the trees will stand (see page 134).

Say: **The roots are the founda-**

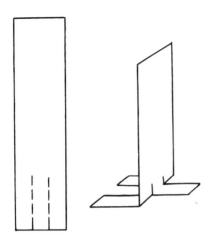

EPHESIANS
4:29-32

THEME:
Be kind to other people and treat them with love.

SUMMARY:
This MUSIC IDEA encourages children to treat people the way Jesus wants us to treat them.

PREPARATION: You'll need a Bible, a box of small cookies or crackers, and a serving tray.

This activity is especially well-suited for young children.

Gather children in a circle on the floor. Ask:

■ **What's the nicest thing someone has done for you?**

■ **How have you been nice to someone else?**

■ **How did it feel when you were nice to that person?**

Say: **God wants us to be kind and loving to one another. We can help others, say nice things to them, and forgive people when they're mean to us. When we treat others the way we want to be treated, everyone is happy. Let's see what the Bible says about how we're to act with others.**

Read aloud Ephesians 4:29-32. Read verse 32 again, then ask:

■ **How does God want us to act toward others?** Encourage children to answer that God wants us to be kind and loving to each other. Challenge each child to name one person they can be kind to during the coming week. Then

tion of a plant or tree. The roots hold trees securely in the ground. Just like trees, our faith needs strong roots to keep it from blowing away or falling down. Who is our foundation? Let's read from the Bible. When you know who our foundation is, put your hand over your heart. Read aloud Ephesians 1:19-23. Encourage children to name Jesus as our foundation. Explain that Jesus is the "root" of our faith.

Have each child tear a green construction paper "treetop." Help children write the word "faith" on the treetops and the name "Jesus" on the roots. Then say: **With Jesus as our strong roots, our faith can blossom and grow. We'll become the good trees the Bible speaks of and will have Jesus as our strong foundation. Use your trees as bookmarks to remind you that our faith is rooted in Jesus.**

have each child tell one way to be kind and loving.

Say: **Let's learn a song to help us remember what the Bible says about treating others with love and kindness.** Sing the following song to the tune of "Ten Little Indians." Children may enjoy hopping around the room and bowing or shaking hands with friends as they sing.

Be kind and loving to each other. *(Bow or shake hands.)*
Be kind and loving to each other. *(Bow or shake hands.)*
Be kind and loving to each other. *(Bow or shake hands.)*
Ephesians 4:32.
(Repeat twice.)

EPHESIANS
6:1-3

THEME:

God wants us to respect our parents and caregivers.

SUMMARY:

This CRAFT idea provides children an opportunity to thank loving parents and caregivers.

PREPARATION: You'll need a Bible, envelopes, scissors, and markers or crayons. If you have access to them, include a variety of rubber stamps and stamp pads with water-soluble ink. You'll also need a photocopy of the "Happy Heart" handout from page 136 for each child plus a few extras for children who wish to make two thank you cards.

TEACHER TIP
Since a traditional family situation may not be representative of each child in your class, be sensitive in allowing children to make separate cards for their parents if they desire.

Set the envelopes, photocopies, and craft supplies on a table. Gather children and ask:
■ **What's the best thing about parents?**
■ **If you could say, "Thank you" to your parent for one thing, what would it be? Why?**
Say: **God has given us a wonderful gift in parents, grandparents, and other loving relatives. God wants us to honor, obey, and respect them. We'll see what the Bible says about the way we should treat our parents.**
Read aloud Ephesians 6:1-3. Then ask:
■ **If you honor and obey your parents, what does God say will happen?**
■ **Why is it important to honor and obey parents?**
■ **Why is it important to express our thanks to loved ones?**
Say: **Today we're going to make special cards to express thanks to parents and loving caregivers.**
Hand each child a photocopy of the "Happy Heart" handout. Show children how to cut out the cards and then decorate the cards with crayons, markers, and the rubber stamps if you chose to use them. Encourage children to color the heart shape red or bright pink. Then demonstrate how to fold the hearts down and the cards in half

HAPPY HEART

Photocopy this page. Cut out the card and decorate it.
Fold the heart inside the card.

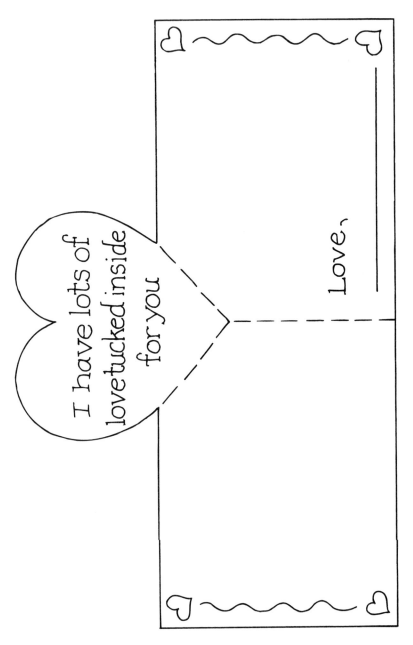

I have lots of love tucked inside for you

Love,

so the hearts are "tucked" inside the cards.

As children work, talk about the kind and loving things parents do. Point out that God gave us parents and caregivers to love us and take care of us. Explain that we're to obey and honor our parents because they know what's best for us.

End the activity with a prayer thanking God for parents. Encourage children to give their cards to parents or other loving relatives.

EPHESIANS
6:10-18

THEME:
We can be strong in the Lord.

SUMMARY:
In this active LEARNING GAME, children learn that God is their protector.

PREPARATION: You'll need a Bible and two each of the following: a cap or hat, a pair of boots, a belt, and a jacket or sweater.

Pile each set of clothing at one end of the room. Gather children at the opposite end and ask:

■ **What articles of clothing or equipment are made to keep you safe?**

■ **What might happen if a baseball umpire forgot to put on his or her face mask and helmet?**

Say: **It's important to stay safe. Sometimes we have to wear special clothing or equipment to keep us safe. Many years ago, knights and soldiers wore suits of shiny armor to protect themselves against arrows and spears. Did you know that God wants us to be safe, too? God wants us to be safe from Satan, so God gives us special armor to wear. Let's read about God's armor. You can help count the pieces of armor on your fingers. Then we'll play a fun game to review how each piece of God's armor keeps us safe.**

Read aloud Ephesians 6:10-18, then ask how many pieces of armor the children counted. Go to one pile of clothing and ask a volunteer to put on each piece of "armor" as you read aloud Ephesians 6:14-17 once more. Explain the significance of each part of the armor of God as the child puts it on. For instance, a cap or hat would be "God's salvation"; a jacket would be the "protection of right living"; a belt would be the "belt of truth"; and boots would be the

"Good News of peace." Have the child hold a Bible as the "sword of the Spirit," and point out that when the Bible is held in front as a shield, it's like the "shield of faith."

When you're finished, have the child return the articles of clothing to the pile. Then have children form two lines at the end of the room opposite the clothing. Say: **Let's play a game. I'll call out a part of God's armor—the "belt of truth," for example. The first person in each line can hop to the clothes, find the belts, and put them on. Then circle twice, take them off, and hop to the back of your line, and I'll call out another piece of the armor.**

Continue playing until each child has had a turn to put on a piece of God's armor.

PHILIPPIANS

"In your lives you must think and act like Christ Jesus."

Philippians 2:5

PHILIPPIANS 2:3-4

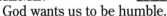

THEME:
God wants us to be humble.

SUMMARY:
This active DEVOTION encourages children not to brag to their friends.

PREPARATION: You'll need Bibles; a bag of large, individually wrapped candies; and a bag of small, individually wrapped candies.

EXPERIENCE

Have the children find partners, and have pairs sit together in a circle. Say: **Some people like to brag. They like to tell others just** how great they are or how much better they are than others. They brag and talk about "me, me, me." We could call that kind of bragging "me bragging." Ask:

■ **What kinds of things would a "me bragger" say?** Let children respond.

Say: **It gets tiring when people "me brag."** But did you know that there's another kind of bragging? We could call it "you bragging." "You bragging" is bragging about another person—telling a person what we appreciate, respect, and admire about him or her. "You bragging" tells people that you're interested in them and that you're proud of who they are and what they do. Ask:

■ **What kinds of things would a "you bragger" say?**

Say: "You braggers" are nice to be around, aren't they? They encourage others and make them feel special. Let's try some "you bragging." Find a partner, and decide who will be the first "you bragger." When I clap my hands, you'll have a few moments to say great things about your partner. When you hear me clap again, switch roles so everyone has a chance to be the "you bragger."

Allow each child at least fifteen seconds to brag about his or her partner.

RESPONSE

After all the children have had a chance to brag about their partners, ask:

■ How did you feel as your partner bragged about you?

■ How is "you bragging" different from "me bragging?"

■ Which kind of bragging do you think God likes? Why?

Say: Let's read what the Bible says about bragging. See if you can tell which kind of bragging is better.

Ask a volunteer to read aloud Philippians 2:3-4. Ask:

■ What does the Bible say about "me bragging"?

■ What does the Bible say about "you bragging"?

Say: If we chose the most important word in this passage, it would be the word "humble." When we're humble, we think less of ourselves and more of others. We honor other people and show them that we're really interested in them. Let's practice thinking more of others.

CLOSING

Set the wrapped candies on a table, and invite children to choose two pieces of candy each: one for themselves and one for their partners.

After everyone has two pieces of candy, say: Look at your candies. Do you have big or little pieces? Chances are that you chose a big piece of candy for yourself—but did you also choose a big piece for your partner? Being selfless and humble means putting others first; it means resisting the urge to brag and to get the best of everything for yourself. It's important to remember that God wants us to be humble. Let's say a prayer asking God to help us be humble. Pray: Dear Lord, please help us remember that it's better to put others first in all we do. Help us resist the urge to "me brag," choosing instead to "you brag." In Jesus' name we pray, amen.

Let children enjoy eating their sweet treats.

PHILIPPIANS 4:4-9

THEME:

We can live as God wants us to live.

SUMMARY:

Use this PARTY to help children recognize the attitudes that Christians need to exhibit in everyday life.

PREPARATION: You'll need Bibles, tape, newsprint, permanent markers, balloons, and the supplies described below for the specific party activities you choose.

Before the party, draw smiling faces on balloons. Be sure to provide a balloon for each child. Also tape a sheet of newsprint to a wall.

Gather children in a circle, and hand each child a colorful balloon. Say: **These balloons look very happy. That's because they know a secret—the secret to being happy Christians. I'm going to read from the Bible. When you hear how to be happy Christians, wave your balloons in the air.**

Read aloud Philippians 4:4-9. Then say: **Look at all the waving balloons! This Bible passage gives us a good list of the kinds of attitudes Christians need to have to be happy Christians. We might call them "happytudes." Let's make a list of the happytudes we just read.**

Help children write the following words on the sheet of newsprint: joy, gentleness, kindness, trust, thankfulness, peace, positive thoughts. Say: **This is quite a list! To show how happy we are being Christians, let's have a party. We'll begin by taping the happy balloons around the room for decorations.** Let children tape their balloons around the room and then enjoy one or more of the following games and activities.

■ Decorate crepe paper streamers with smiling faces.

■ Run a Jolly-Joy Relay in which teams race to a chalkboard to write the names of people or places that bring them joy.

■ Exchange "kindness coupons" with which children promise to do something kind for others—sweeping the floor or washing the dishes, for example.

■ Have each child write his or her name on a paper plate. Then have children sit in a circle and pass their plates around the circle, writing a special message to each child on his or her plate. After each child's plate has completed the circle, let the children read and enjoy their keepsake plates.

■ Have a songfest with lots of clapping and foot-stomping using joyous praise songs such as "Joyful, Joyful, We Adore Thee," "If You're Happy and You Know It," "Trust and Obey," "I've Got Peace Like a River," and "Let There Be Peace on Earth."

■ For a festive snack, serve apple juice and cupcakes decorated with smiling faces.

COLOSSIANS

"Do all these things; but most important, love each other. Love is what holds you all together in perfect unity."

Colossians 3:14

COLOSSIANS 1:11

THEME:
God strengthens our patience.

SUMMARY:
Use this OBJECT LESSON to help children discover that they can count on God to help them "keep on keeping on."

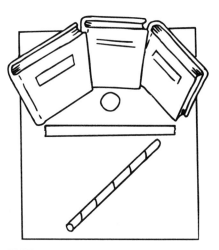

PREPARATION: You'll need a Bible, drinking straws, a pingpong ball, masking tape, a vacuum cleaner with hose attachment, and three books.

On a flat surface, create a three-sided "cage" by standing three books on end. Place a strip of masking tape in front of the open side of the cage.

Have the children form two groups, and hand a drinking straw to each child. Place a pingpong ball at the back of the cage. Ask one group to try drawing the ball out of the cage and across the masking tape line by sucking on the straws.

Tell children that drinking straws cannot cross the masking tape line. After the first group tries the task for a minute, have the other group try.

After both groups have had a turn, let each try again using the vacuum cleaner hose attachment. Again, tell the children to be sure the hose doesn't cross the masking tape line. After both groups have had a turn, ask:

■ **Why was this activity frustrating the first time?**

■ **Were you tempted to give up? Explain.**

■ **How did you feel when the power of the vacuum cleaner was added?**

■ **How was this activity like relying on God's power to help us?**

Say: **We're often faced with situations that are frustrating and that make us feel impatient. We might even feel like giving up. But we know that God's power can strengthen us, helping us to keep trying. Let's see what the Bible says about relying on God's power to help us.**

Have the children form a circle, and have a volunteer read aloud Colossians 1:11. Then ask:

■ **Why does God want to strengthen us?**

Say: **Let's pass a pingpong ball around the circle. When you hold the ball, name a problem you have that God's strength could help you overcome. After the ball has made it all the way around the circle, we'll all say together, "Have patience—trust in God!"**

Have the children pass the pingpong ball around the circle until everyone has had a turn naming a problem.

Say: **There are lots of things we can't do through our own strength, and that's OK because we know that God is always ready to help us have patience and keep trying. Let's say a prayer and ask God to help us have patience.**

Pray: **Dear God, please give us the patience to hang in there with problems. Help us remember that we can count on your power to help us solve our problems. In Jesus' name, amen.**

Send the drinking straws home with children as reminders that although their power may not be enough to overcome problems, God's power is.

COLOSSIANS 1:16

THEME:
God is the only creator.

SUMMARY:
Use this SKIT to teach children that all things were made by God and for God.

GOD SPOKE

SCENE: Things on earth are coming to life as God creates the world.

PROPS: Although no props are necessary, you could present a more elaborate skit by creating costumes and props for the characters to use.

Before the skit, have children get into groups of one or more. You'll need Trees, Sky, Birds, Fish, Animals, and People groups.

Instruct group members to silently act out their parts as Reader 1 and Reader 2 narrate.

CHARACTERS:
Reader 1
Trees
Sky
Fish
Birds
Animals
People
Reader 2

SCRIPT

(Character groups are scattered about the stage. Characters are crouched on the floor, waiting for their cues.)

Reader 1: God made our world. He spoke, and everything from tiny spiders to lumbering elephants came into being. God spoke, and seeds appeared. They grew into tall trees.
(Trees stand and stretch as if growing.)

Reader 1: There were apple trees with crunchy fruit, maple trees with sticky sap, and even palm trees with sweet coconuts.
(Trees improvise actions for the different kinds of fruit they bear.)

Reader 1: God told the trees to make more seeds so there would be trees and plants everywhere.
(Trees freeze in place.)

Reader 1: God spoke, and the sky filled with stars: shooting stars, bright stars, distant stars, twinkling stars.
(Members of the Sky group wiggle their fingers and wave their arms to represent twinkling or shooting stars.)

Reader 1: God made a big, bright light to watch over the day and a smaller light to watch over the night.
(Members of the Sky group improvise actions for the sun and moon.)

Reader 1: The sun gave light so the plants would grow, and the moon gently glowed throughout the night.
(Members of the Sky group freeze in place.)

Reader 1: God spoke, and the oceans, rivers, and lakes teemed with fish: sharp-toothed sharks and enormous whales, sea horses and smiling dolphins.
(Fish "swim" around.)

Reader 1: The water was alive with scales, flippers, fins, and tentacles!
(Fish freeze in place.)

Reader 1: God spoke, and birds flapped their feathery wings.
(Birds flap their arms.)

Reader 1: There were long-legged storks, squatty penguins, twittering songbirds, and tappity-tapping woodpeckers.
(Birds imitate the different birds and their sounds.)

Reader 1: They built nests in the trees, in the ground, or in the grass that grew along the river banks. And when the birds laid eggs, the earth was filled with more and more birds.
(Birds freeze in place.)

Reader 1: God spoke, and animals covered the earth.
(Animals act out various parts.)

Reader 1: Grumbly lions, tail-wagging dogs, gentle deer, snazzy zebras... God made everything that walked, hopped, crawled, slithered, and galloped! Animals hung from trees, waded in mud,

145 COLOSSIANS ■

---

burrowed in the ground, and hid behind rocks. The earth became a busy place!

(All the groups except the People move for a few moments, then freeze in place.)

Reader 1: But God wasn't finished yet. God spoke again and created people. God made people in his image.

(People scatter around the other groups.)

Reader 1: God gave them fingers and toes, hair and eyelashes. God gave them the ability to sneeze, laugh, hiccup, and yawn. But most important of all, God gave people *(pause)* love! He made people to love him. God made you and I to love him.

Reader 2: "Through his power all things were made—things in heaven and on earth, things seen and unseen, all powers, authorities, lords, and rulers. All things were made through Christ and for Christ" Colossians 1:16.

Permission to photocopy this skit from *The Children's Worker's Encyclopedia of Bible-Teaching Ideas: NT* granted for local church use. Copyright © Group Publishing, Inc., P.O. Box 481, Loveland, CO 80539.

If you use this skit as a discussion starter, here are possible questions:

■ **In what ways are people different from the other things God created?**

■ **How does it feel to know that God made us in his image?**

■ **What does it mean that we were made to love God?**

■ **How can our lives show that we love God?**

COLOSSIANS 3:8-10

THEME:
We can have new lives with Jesus.

SUMMARY:
Use this CRAFT project to help children discover that Christ gives them new life by changing their hearts.

PREPARATION: You'll need a Bible, colored construction paper, white paper, scissors, markers, tape, and a picture of Jesus or a sheet of poster board.

Before this activity, tape the picture of Jesus to a wall, door, or bulletin board. If you don't have a picture of Jesus, write his name on a sheet of poster board and hang it on the wall.

Have children form pairs, and hand each pair two sheets of colored construction paper, two sheets of white paper, a marker, and scissors. Have each child help his or her partner trace and cut out a white footprint and a colored footprint.

After all the footprints have been cut out, say: **It's not always easy to follow in Jesus' footsteps. Sometimes we're tempted to do or say the wrong things—then we're off on the "wrong foot."** Ask:

■ **What are some things that keep people from following Jesus?**

Say: **With your partners, think**

of two ways people stray from Jesus; then write those ways on your colored footprints. If your class includes children who cannot write, have them draw pictures or dictate their thoughts to someone older. After everyone has prepared a colored footprint, invite children to tape their footprints near the picture of Jesus. Position the paper footprints so they appear to be "walking" to Christ.

Read aloud Colossians 3:8-10. Then say: **This Scripture tells us that with Jesus in our lives, we don't have to walk in the old ways we used to walk. We have new life through Jesus, and we can walk on a new path, too. Jesus helps us leave our old, sinful ways and turn to good,** new ways of living. Ask:

■ **What are some of the new, good things we have in our new lives with Jesus?** Help children think of things such as love, honesty, forgiveness, kindness, trust, faith, and hope. Have each child write one of these words on his or her white footprint and then tape that footprint "walking" away from the picture of Jesus.

Have a time of silence during which the children think of ways they'd like to follow Jesus more closely. Then close with this prayer: **Dear God, we thank you for giving us new life through Jesus. Help us remember that we can walk in Jesus' love and forgiveness and that we have new lives in Jesus. Amen.**

1 THESSALONIANS

"Also, we always thank God because when you heard his message from us, you accepted it as the word of God, not the words of humans. And it really is God's message which works in you who believe."

1 Thessalonians 2:13

1 THESSALONIANS 4:9-11

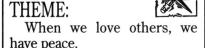

THEME:
When we love others, we have peace.

SUMMARY:
In this CRAFT activity, children learn that God replaces conflict with peace.

PREPARATION: You'll need a Bible, old map or atlas pages, poster board, ribbon, tape, and scissors.

Before this activity, cut an eight-inch length of ribbon for each child. You'll also need to cut a dove from poster board for each child using the dove pattern provided.

Set out old map or atlas pages, scissors, tape, and the lengths of ribbon.

Hand each child a poster board dove. Ask:

■ **Does anyone know what the symbol of a dove means?**

Say: **Doves are sometimes rec-**

ognized as symbols of peace. We'd like to live in a world full of doves and peace, but our world has a lot of troubles and conflicts in it. People argue and disagree, and there seem to be fights all over the world every day. But God has a way to make peace. Let's read what the Bible tells us about living peaceably.

Have a volunteer read aloud 1 Thessalonians 4:9-11. Ask:

■ **Who does God want us to love?**

■ **How can loving others give peace to us? to the world?**

■ **Where do we get the strength to forgive and love others?**

■ **How can we show others our love? our forgiveness?**

Say: **God wants us to do everything possible to live in peace with other people in our families, in our towns, and all around the world. We can make peaceful bookmarks to remind us that love makes peace around the world.**

Show children how to cut or tear map pages into hearts smaller than the paper dove shapes. Have children tape the hearts to their paper doves. Then have each child tape a length of ribbon to the back of each dove to make a bookmark.

End the activity with this prayer: **Dear God, we thank you for the gift of peace that comes from your love. Help us love others and spread peace around the world. In Jesus' name, amen.**

1 THESSALONIANS 5:14-15

THEME:
God wants us to care for others.

SUMMARY:
With this SERVICE PROJECT, children discover ways to care for people who need help.

PREPARATION: You'll need a Bible, markers, colored construction paper, glue sticks, poster board, and a large box. You'll also need a clean, used blanket to donate.

Before class, write the following phrase in big block letters on the poster board: "Jesus' love will cover you!"

Set out the large box, the glue sticks, and the colored construction paper in one corner of the room. In another area, set out a sheet of poster board and colorful markers.

Gather children in the center of the room. Say: **We know that Jesus came to help people—especially people who were afraid or weak. Jesus wanted them to know that he was their friend and would love and care for them. Remember when Jesus calmed the storm for the frightened disciples? Or when Jesus fed five thousand hungry people? These are good examples of how Jesus cared for people.** Ask:

■ **Does Jesus want us to care for others? How do you know?**

■ **What are ways we can care for people who are afraid? weak?**

hungry? homeless?

Say: **Let's read what the Bible says about caring for others.** Ask a volunteer to read aloud 1 Thessalonians 5:14-15. Then ask:

■ **Who does God want us to help?**

■ **How are we to help these people?** Encourage children to name the ways suggested in the Scripture passage: encouragement and patience.

Say: **It's important to know that we can help others through the love Jesus puts in our hearts. In this way, we can spread the warmth of Jesus' love to many people.** Hold up the blanket. **Just as this blanket covers people and keeps them warm, Jesus' love covers them. Let's help some people who need real warmth by having a "Big Blanket Cover-Up" drive. We'll work to donate blankets and warm quilts to homeless or needy people to keep them warm.**

Have the children form two groups: the Box Builders and the Sign Designers. Say: **The Box Builders can work to decorate the large box with colorful scraps of construction paper. We'll use the box to hold the blankets we collect. The Sign Designers can use the poster board and markers to create a giant card to accompany the blankets. Then during the next two weeks, you can bring in new or clean used blankets and quilts to donate. At the end of two weeks, we'll have someone from the church take our box of blankets and card to a homeless shelter so people can cover up with their new blankets—and with lots of love!**

If possible, arrange for the children to ride along when the blankets are delivered.

2 THESSALONIANS

"So, brothers and sisters, stand strong and continue to believe the teachings we gave you in our speaking and in our letter."

2 Thessalonians 2:15

---

2 THESSALONIANS 2:16-17

THEME:
God encourages us.

SUMMARY:
This CRAFT project reminds children that God's encouragement is for real—and for everyone!

PREPARATION: You'll need a Bible, yarn, scissors, tape, a bag of three- to five-inch nails, and a disposable plastic plate for each child. You'll find thin plastic plates beside the paper plates in the picnic or paper-goods section of most grocery stores.

Before class, cut the inside circles from the plastic plates to create plas-tic rings. Prepare a ring for each child. Also, be sure you have at least four nails for each child; the more nails per child, the better. If you have younger children in class, use large jingle bells instead of nails. You may want to pre-cut the yarn into ten-inch lengths and twelve-inch lengths. You'll need at least four ten-inch pieces and four twelve-inch pieces of yarn for each child.

Set the nails or jingle bells, plastic rings, yarn, and tape on a table.

Have the children form three groups, and have the groups go to separate areas of the room. Ask Group 1 to discuss times they've felt discouraged because some important job seemed impossible to do.

Ask Group 2 to discuss times they've been discouraged because nobody noticed something nice they had done for someone else.

Ask Group 3 to discuss times they've been discouraged because nobody noticed something nice they said to someone.

After several minutes of discussion, call the groups together. Say: **We've all felt discouraged at some time or another. And what we need when we're feeling discouraged is a quick dose of encouragement. We need encouragement in our lives as much as we need food, air, and water. Encouragement helps us keep trying to do good things for God. The Apostle Paul knew how important encouragement is. He even wrote a little prayer about it.**

Ask a volunteer to read aloud 2 Thessalonians 2:16-17. Say: **We can always count on God's encouragement when we're doing or saying something good.**

God's encouragement is a bit like the wind: We may not be able to see it, but we see what it does. God's encouragement gives us energy and confidence to keep on keeping on! We can work for God longer, tell more people we love God, and spread his love and encouragement to others. Let's make wind chimes to remind us that God's encouragement is as real as the wind.

Let children work in pairs or trios. Demonstrate how to tie a nail to the end of each piece of yarn, then tape the yarn around the edges of the plastic rings. Help young children tie large jingle bells to the ends of the yarn instead of nails.

Be sure each child has attached at least four nails to his or her wind chime. Tape four twelve-inch pieces of yarn to the plastic ring, then tie the yarn at the top to make a hanger.

Invite the children to bring their wind chimes into a prayer circle. Encourage them to blow gently on the chimes as you offer this prayer: **Dear God, we're glad that your encouragement is as real as the wind. And we're thankful that we can count on your encouragement to help us. In Jesus' name, amen.**

Tell children to hang their wind chimes in a window or on a patio to remind them of God's powerful encouragement.

2 THESSALONIANS 3:2-3

THEME:
God is faithful.

SUMMARY:
This OBJECT LESSON helps children understand that they can rely on God's protection.

PREPARATION: You'll need Bibles, leaves, a brick, paper, and pencils. This activity also requires a warm, sunny day and access to a garden hose.

Ask the children to retell the story of the three little pigs. After the story, ask:
■ **Why didn't the house of straw or sticks protect the little pigs from the big, bad wolf?**
■ **Why couldn't the wolf blow down the house of bricks?**

Say: **Most of us don't find ourselves threatened by big, bad wolves. But we are often threatened by bad thoughts, mean words from others, hurtful things others do to us, and even the temptation to say and do wrong things ourselves. Let's take a look at how we're protected from bad things.**

Let each child find a leaf. Say: **These leaves represent us.** Then hold up the garden hose and say: **This water hose represents the big, bad wolves in our lives. Let's take turns laying our leaves on the ground and seeing what happens to us when bad things come along.**

Turn on the hose, and let the water push the leaves aside. Ask:
■ **How is the way the water pushes the leaves like the way we get pushed and hurt when no one protects us?**
■ **Do you think there's someone who can protect us from bad things in life? Explain.**

Say: **God knows that bad things threaten us every day. And God loves us enough to** help us with those bad things. **Here's a brick that we can pretend is God's protection. Let's see what happens when God covers us with his protection.** Place the brick on a leaf, and turn on the water. After a few moments, say: **See? God's protection covers us. Now let's see what the Bible says about God's protection.**

Have the children form groups of four. Give each group a Bible, a piece of paper, and a pencil. Within each group, appoint a Reader, a Recorder, a Checker, and a Reporter. Explain that the Reader will read aloud the Bible passage, the Recorder will write down the thoughts of the group, the Checker will make sure that the group agrees on what is written, and the Reporter will report back to the large group.

Ask each group to do the following:
■ read 2 Thessalonians 3:2-3,
■ discuss times they've felt threatened, and
■ list ways that God protects us.

After several minutes, have the Reporters read their group's list of how God protects us. Then say: **Just as the brick covered the leaf, God's protection covers us. God protects us with his powerful love, and we can rely on that!**

Close with a time of quiet reflection. Encourage children to think of times they've felt God's protection. Then say this prayer: **Dear God, thank you for your loving protection. We're so glad we know your protection is always with us. In Jesus' name, amen.**

1 TIMOTHY

"Do not let anyone treat you as if you are unimportant because you are young. Instead, be an example to the believers with your words, your actions, your love, your faith, and your pure life."

1 Timothy 4:12

1 TIMOTHY 1:12-16

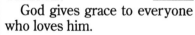

THEME:
God gives grace to everyone who loves him.

SUMMARY:
Use this active DEVOTION to help children understand the concept of grace.

PREPARATION: You'll need Bibles, a box of round crackers, paper lunch sacks, and a sign made from poster board that says "Bank."

EXPERIENCE

Hand each child a paper lunch sack, and tell children that the sacks are their "money bags."

Place the "Bank" sign and several stacks of crackers on a table. Say: **This is a pretend bank with stacks of make-believe money. I'll be the banker. I'll call you to the bank, and then I'll give you each one "coin" for your money bag. Don't let anyone peek into your money bag after your trip to the bank.** Call each child to the bank, but instead of one cracker coin, give each child a small handful of coins. If your class is very large, you may wish to use popcorn or oyster crackers as coins.

RESPONSE

After everyone has gone to the bank, ask:
■ **How did you feel when you received a lot of coins instead of just one?**
■ **Why do you think you re-**

ceived more than you expected?

■ **How does it make you feel to know that everyone received more than they expected?**

As children munch their crunchy coins, say: **You only expected one coin, but instead, you received many. And you didn't have to work for those coins or earn them. That's the way God's grace works. God gives us his grace and love as free gifts, and he always gives us more than we can imagine. Let's see what the Bible says about God's grace.**

Group the children in pairs, placing nonreaders with readers. Have someone in each pair read aloud 1 Timothy 1:12-16. Then ask:

■ **What kinds of bad things did Paul do before he knew the Lord?**

■ **Do you think Paul deserved God's grace? Explain.**

■ **How did Paul's life change after he received God's grace?** Help the children understand that Paul began to serve the Lord and love him. Point out that Paul told many others about Jesus and God and about their love.

Say: **Paul didn't have to pay a thing for God's grace—and neither do we. God's grace is a free gift that can change our lives forever.**

CLOSING

Have the children form two groups. Have the groups stand in intersecting lines to form a "prayer cross." Encourage children to think about one thing in their lives they'd like God to help them change. Close with this prayer: **Dear Lord, please help us accept the gift of your grace. There are things in**

our lives we'd like to change, and we need your help and love and grace to change them. Thank you for making your grace available to everyone and for loving us as you do. In Jesus' name, amen.

1 TIMOTHY 2:1-3

THEME:
We can pray for others.

SUMMARY:
Use this QUIET REFLECTION to help children realize that they can intercede for others with prayer.

PREPARATION: You'll need a Bible, five sheets of newsprint, markers, and masking tape.

Gather children and ask:
■ **What is prayer?**

■ **What things do you pray for?**

■ **How important do you think it is for Christians to pray for others? Explain.**

Say: **God always hears our prayers, and he answers them in his time and in his own way. Many prayers we pray are for ourselves, but did you know that we're supposed to pray for others, too? We can find out what the Bible says about praying for others.**

Ask a volunteer to read aloud 1 Timothy 2:1-3. Ask:
■ **Who are we to pray for?**

■ Have you ever prayed for someone? Tell us what happened.

Say: **When we pray for others, we ask God for things they need or we ask God to help care for those people. Today we're going to think of people who could use our prayers. Then we'll pray for them.**

Have the children form five small groups. Hand each group a piece of newsprint and a marker. Say: **You'll have a few minutes to list the names of people your group would like to pray for and why they need prayer. For example, Mrs. Smith might need prayer for her hurt ankle or Sam might need prayer because bullies are teasing him. You can include family members, friends, teachers, people in our government, or even people you might not get along with. Write their names on your papers; then we'll have a time of prayer.**

Allow several minutes for children to make their prayer lists. Then say: **Put your prayer list in the center of your group so each person can see it. I'll begin to say a prayer. When I leave room for people's names, quietly whisper the names on your list. And when I leave space for their needs, quietly tell those needs. Now let's fold our hands for prayer.** Pray. **Dear God, we're glad that we can pray for others and that you hear those prayers. Today we'd like to pray for** (insert people's names). **This person needs prayer for** (insert the people's prayer needs). **We thank you, God, that you hear each** prayer and that you answer each prayer, too. Help us remember to pray for others. In Jesus' name, amen.

1 TIMOTHY 4:11-12

THEME:
We're never too young to model Christ's love.

SUMMARY:
Use this SKIT to teach children that they can model Christ's love even though they're young.

PREPARATION: You'll need a Bible, five sheets of newsprint, markers, and masking tape.

LITTLE SISTER LEADS

SCENE: anywhere

PROPS: none

Before the skit, have children form three groups to cooperatively act out each character: Big Brother, Middle Brother, and Little Sister. If you have a mixed-age class, group children according to their ages, creating an oldest group, a middle group, and a youngest group. If you choose, you may be the Reader and direct children to act out the skit as you read it.

CHARACTERS:
Reader
Big Brother
Middle Brother
Little Sister

SCRIPT

Reader: Once upon a time, there was a Big Brother *(Big Brother group waves)*, a Middle Brother *(Middle Brother group waves)*, and a Little Sister. *(Little Sister group waves.)* As happens in many families, the younger brother and sister copied what their older brother did. If the Big Brother tried surfing *(Big Brother group pretends to surf)*, the Middle Brother and Little Sister would try it, too. *(Middle Brother and Little Sister groups imitate Big Brother.)* If the Big Brother was into ballet dancing, *(Big Brother group dances a silly ballet-style dance)*, you can be sure that the Middle Brother and Little Sister would soon be twirling on their toes. *(Middle Brother and Little Sister groups leap and twirl.)*

And so it went, through playing the guitar *(Big Brother group strums "air guitars," then Middle Brother and Little Sister groups imitate)*, eating corn on the cob *(repeat action pattern)*, talking on the phone *(repeat pattern)*, and even acting like a monkey *(repeat again)*.

But one day, things began to change. The Little Sister decided to give her friends high fives. *(Little Sister group members give each other high fives.)* The Middle Brother watched his Little Sister and saw how much her friends liked the high fives, so he gave high fives to his friends, too. *(Middle Brother group members give each other high fives.)* When the Big Brother saw what Middle Brother and Little Sister were doing, he started giving his friends high fives, too! *(Big Brother group imitates the younger groups.)* What was going on? Then the Little Sister started scratching her friends' backs because she knew it was a nice thing to do. *(Little Sister group members gently scratch each other's backs.)* Before long, Middle Brother and Big Brother saw how nice it was, and they started doing scratching, too. *(Big Brothers and Middle Brothers scratch each other's backs.)*

From that day on, Big Brother and Middle Brother followed Little Sister's example. They realized that her age didn't matter because her examples of kindness were so great! *(Little Sister group waves to the audience; then the Middle and Big Brother groups imitate by waving as everyone exits.)*

If you use this skit as a discussion starter, here are possible questions:

■ **How can you model Christ's love for others to follow?**

■ **Why does age sometimes hold us back from helping others know and love Jesus?**

■ **Who can you model Christ's love for?**

2 TIMOTHY

"All Scripture is given by God and is useful for teaching, for showing people what is wrong in their lives, for correcting faults, and for teaching how to live right."

2 Timothy 3:16

2 TIMOTHY
1:6-12

THEME:
Don't be afraid to spread the good news.

SUMMARY:
Use this MUSIC IDEA to help children discover the joy of spreading the good news of Jesus Christ's love.

PREPARATION: You'll need Bibles, a cassette recorder, tape, a pen, and newsprint. You'll also need a new, blank cassette tape.

Have the children form groups of four, pairing older children with younger ones. Say: **Let's play a little game to get us warmed up. I'll hum a song. When you know the name of the song, put your hands on your head.** Begin to hum a familiar song, such as "Jesus Loves Me" or "Away in a Manger." When almost everyone's hands are on their heads, stop humming and say: **Good for you! Now let's see if you can get this one!** Hum another song until children recognize it. Then say: **You're pretty good at recognizing songs.** Ask:

■ **How do songs make you feel?**

■ **Why do you think people remember songs so easily?**

Say: **Songs are a great way to remember important things or words. For example, how many of you learned the letters to the** alphabet through singing the alphabet song? Pause for response. And did you know that singing or humming songs are great ways to tell others about Jesus and about God's love? Ask:

■ Why is it good to tell others about Jesus?

■ Do you think Jesus wants us to tell others about him? Explain.

Say: Let's get into small groups and see what the Bible says about telling others the good news about Jesus. Have children form groups of four and choose one or two readers for each group.

Hand a Bible to each small group, and circulate as children read aloud 2 Timothy 1:6-12. After all the groups have finished reading, ask:

■ Who is supposed to tell the good news about Jesus?

■ Are we ever to be afraid to tell others about Jesus? Why not?

■ What are some ways we can share the good news of Jesus?

After the children have offered their suggestions, say: One of the happiest ways to share the good news about Jesus is through music. We know a lot of songs about Jesus. Suppose we were to make a recording of some of those songs. What ones might we want to record? Let's write them on this paper.

Tape a piece of newsprint to the wall, and write down children's suggestions for song titles. Then have a songfest, and record the children singing each song. You may wish to sing each song through once or twice before recording it. Consider using a musical background tape or even asking someone from the congregation with musical talent to accompany your "concert."

After the songs have been recorded, have the children sign their names as "recording artists" on the small card that comes inside the plastic cassette tape box. List the songs in order on the card as well.

Let the child whose birthday is coming up soonest take the tape to share with someone during the coming week. The following week, the child with the next closest birthday can borrow the tape for sharing, and so on.

Each time a child returns the tape, encourage that child to tell who he or she shared the tape with and how that person responded to the songs. Also ask that child to describe how he or she felt sharing the good news of Jesus.

Consider making extra copies of the tape for each child to take home as a keepsake.

2 TIMOTHY 3:1-5

THEME:
God wants us to choose good friends.

SUMMARY:
Use this LEARNING GAME to help children recognize the importance of choosing good friends.

PREPARATION: You'll need a Bible, construction paper, markers, magnets, metal paper clips, string, a yardstick, and a bedsheet.

Before class, attach a magnet to the end of a two-foot piece of string. Tie the other end of the string onto the end of the yardstick.

Have children form two groups, then hand each child a piece of construction paper and a marker. Have each child tear one fish shape from the construction paper. Ask one group to brainstorm about the characteristics of a good friend and then to write a different characteristic on the side of each of their fish. Ask the other group to do the same but with the characteristics of a bad friend.

When the children are finished writing on their fish, collect the markers. Invite the children to read aloud the characteristics of good and bad friends from their fish. Ask children to explain why they chose those particular characteristics.

Pass out paper clips. Have each child slide a paper clip onto the tail of his or her fish. Then collect the fish, and place them on the bedsheet "sea." Have children sit around the sea, then say: **We all enjoy having friends, but God wants us to have the right kind of friends. Let's see what the Bible says about the friends we should have.** Have volunteers read aloud 2 Timothy 3:1-5. Briefly discuss similarities and differences between negative and positive characteristics of friends and how they compare with the lists that the children wrote on their fish. Then ask:

■ **What does this passage say we should do about people who disobey their parents or gossip or refuse to forgive others?**

■ **Why is it important to choose good friends?**

Say: **Finding good friends isn't always easy. It's a little like fishing—sometimes you catch a real winner, and sometimes it's best to throw your catch back into the sea! Let's have some fun going fishing for friends. We'll take turns using this special "fishing pole."** Hold up the yardstick fishing pole. **Any fish on which the characteristic of a good friend is written is a "keeper," and you can keep the fish. The other fish must be thrown back into the sea.**

If a child catches more than one "keeper," have the child offer to give the fish to someone who hasn't caught a keeper.

TITUS

"He gave himself for us so he might pay the price to free us from all evil and to make us pure people who belong only to him—people who are always wanting to do good deeds."

Titus 2:14

TITUS 2:7-14

THEME:
God wants us to help others.

SUMMARY:
Use this SERVICE PROJECT to help children become sensitive to the needs of others.

PREPARATION: You'll need a Bible. If the weather is suitable for outdoor work around the church, you'll need rakes, brooms, and garbage bags. If the weather is unsuitable for outdoor work, you'll need indoor cleaning supplies such as dust cloths, paper towels, feather dusters, window cleaner, and a vacuum.

Before planning your day of service, contact the appropriate church staff to ask permission.

Gather children in a group and ask:
■ **Who keeps your yard and house in tiptop shape?**
■ **How do you think that person would feel if he or she had help keeping things nice?**
■ **Who keeps the church and our churchyard looking nice?**
■ **Why is it good to help others?**
Say: **We know that it's a fine thing to help others. But what do you think God says about helping out? We can find out by reading the Bible.**
Have a volunteer read aloud Titus 2:7-14. Then read aloud Titus 2:14 once more. Ask:
■ **What are good deeds you**

can do for someone this week?

Say: Another word for good deeds is "service." Christians want to serve others just as Jesus served people. Ask:

■ Who serves people in our church?

■ How does each person in our church serve others?

■ Why is it our Christian responsibility to serve others?

Say: The people at our church do many things for us, don't they? Let's give some of that service back to the people of our church. We can have a church cleanup day and work to clean the yard or spiff up the inside of the church.

Announce when you'll do your service project. Tell the children to wear old clothes so they can dig into the project.

PHILEMON

*"So, my brother, I ask that you do this for me
in the Lord: Refresh my heart in Christ."*

Philemon 20

PHILEMON
4-17

THEME:
God wants us to accept others.

SUMMARY:
Use this fun CREATIVE STORY-TELLING activity to retell the story of Paul and Onesimus and to help children discover the depth of Christian friendship and acceptance.

PREPARATION: You'll need a Bible, markers, and balloons.
Before this activity, inflate and tie off a balloon for each child.

Gather children into three groups and ask:

■ Has a friend of yours ever been in trouble? How did you feel?

■ Would you take a friend's punishment for something he or she did? Why or why not?

Say: **Friends are precious gifts from God. The Apostle Paul had a friend named Onesimus** (oh-NES-ih-mus). **Guess what Paul wanted to do? He wanted to take the punishment for something his friend had done. Let's hear this special Bible story of friendship. You can help tell the story with these balloons.** Have each group form a standing circle, and hand a balloon to each child. Point to one group and say: **This group has Paul balloons.** Point to another group and say: **This group has Onesimus balloons.** Point to the third group and say:

And this group has Philemon balloons. When I say the name of your balloon person, raise your balloon high into the air and then hold it in front of you again. Ready?

Tell the following Bible story, pausing after each character name to allow children to raise and lower their balloons.

Open the Bible to Philemon 4-17 to show the children where the story comes from. Then say: **Once long ago, there was a man named Philemon. He was a Christian, but he owned many servants. One of the servants was named Onesimus. Onesimus wasn't a Christian, and he stole things from his master, Philemon; then he ran away.**

After he ran away, Onesimus became a Christian. Onesimus knew that he had done a bad thing when he stole from his master, Philemon. Onesimus knew that he should go back and apologize, but Onesimus also knew that he might be punished severely if he returned to his master.

The Apostle Paul was a friend to Philemon, and Paul was in prison for serving Jesus. While in prison, Paul met the runaway slave Onesimus, the two became friends, and Paul taught Onesimus about Jesus.

Paul wanted to help Onesimus, so he wrote a letter to Philemon, the master. Paul asked Philemon to forgive Onesimus. Paul told Philemon how Onesimus had become a Christian and loved Jesus with all his heart. Since Onesimus was Paul's friend, Paul wanted Philemon to be Onesimus' friend and brother in Christ, too. Paul didn't want Onesimus to be punished—in fact, Paul offered to receive Onesimus' punishment himself!

Paul wanted Philemon to love and accept Onesimus as a Christian friend. He wanted Philemon to love Onesimus as Jesus loved them.

Have children hold their balloons. Ask:

■ Why was Paul was so nice to Onesimus?

■ Do you think Philemon listened to Paul and accepted Onesimus? Explain.

Say: **This is a great story about Christian friends accepting one another as Jesus accepted us. I'm sure we can all think of friends we'd like to tell about Jesus. I'm going to hand each of you a marker. On your balloon, write the name of at least one person you can tell about Jesus this week. Then we'll say a prayer as we bop our balloons in the air.**

Let children write names on their balloons, then set the markers aside. Form a circle, and as children gently bop their balloons up and down, offer the following prayer: **Dear Lord, thank you for friends and for the chance to tell them about Jesus. Help us accept our friends as they are and encourage them to accept others with Jesus' love. In his name, amen.**

Let children take their balloons home as reminders to tell their friends about Jesus.

HEBREWS

"God's word is alive and working and is sharper than a double-edged sword. It cuts all the way into us, where the soul and the spirit are joined, to the center of our joints and bones. And it judges the thoughts and feelings in our hearts."

Hebrews 4:12

HEBREWS 1:1-12

THEME:
Jesus reflects the glory of God.

SUMMARY:
This creative PRAYER helps children realize that knowing Jesus helps them know more about God.

PREPARATION: You'll need a Bible, a mirror, and a basin of water. You'll also need a small pebble for each child in class. Because of the small pebbles, this devotion is safest for children over six years of age.

Stand with your back to the children and hold a mirror up. Look at the children through the mirror and describe their actions and appearances. For example, you might say, "I see Martin's red tie" or "I see that Jessica is scratching her arm." After a few observations, ask:

■ **How can I see what you're doing or what you're wearing?**

■ **What does it mean when we say that a mirror reflects something or someone?** Lead children to explain that when something is reflected, an image is shone back.

Say: **Did you know that Jesus is like a beautiful reflection of God? When we learn about Jesus and what he was like, we're also learning more about God. Let's see what the Bible** says about Jesus reflecting God's glory.

Have volunteers read aloud Hebrews 1:1-12. Then say: **If Jesus shows us what God is like, then all we have to do to know God better is to know Jesus. So let's think about what we know about Jesus.** Ask:

■ **Who was Jesus?**

■ **Was he proud or humble? How do you know?**

■ **Was he friendly? What makes you think so?**

■ **Did he care for others or was he selfish? Explain.**

■ **Was he honest? How do you know?**

■ **Could Jesus do anything? Explain.**

Hand a pebble to each child; then invite the children to gather around the basin of water. Gently place the mirror at the bottom of the basin so it reflects upward.

Say: **This mirror will reflect our pebbles just as Jesus reflects God and just as we can reflect Jesus' love and kindness.** Invite a child to drop his or her pebble into the basin while praying, "Jesus, help me reflect your love as you reflect God's love." When the ripples from that pebble have died away, invite the next child to take a turn.

After all the children have prayed and dropped a pebble in the water, close with this prayer: **Thank you, God, for sending Jesus into the world to show us what you're like. Help us learn more about Jesus so we may know more about you, too. In Jesus' name, amen.**

HEBREWS 3:12-13

THEME:
God wants us to encourage others.

SUMMARY:
This AFFIRMATION ACTIVITY helps children recognize the need to affirm the good in others.

PREPARATION: You'll need a Bible, scraps of pink or red felt, scissors, tape, self-adhesive labels, and markers. You'll also need a large, smooth rock.

Have a volunteer read aloud Hebrews 3:12-13. Then slowly draw the outline of a heart on the rock. Ask:

■ **Did you ever hear the expression "He has a hard heart?" or "She has a hard heart?" What do you think it means?**

■ **Do you know anybody who might have a hard heart? What is that person like?**

■ **What does the Bible say is dangerous about having a hard heart?**

Say: **People with hard hearts are people who have turned away from God. They are usually unfeeling and uncaring and uninterested in doing what God wants us to do.** Ask:

■ **Why do you think people might turn away from God?**

■ **What can we do to keep people from getting hard hearts?**

Lead children to understand that we can encourage people to stay near to God.

Say: **The word "encourage" actually means "to make brave."** If we encourage others, we help to make them brave so they can stand up to temptation. If we don't encourage them, they may give in to temptation.

Point to the rock with the heart outline on it. Say: **This rock is like a hard heart. What we need and want are soft hearts—hearts that are open and loving to God.**

Hand a piece of pink or red felt to each child. Help children cut out hearts from the pieces of felt. After everyone has finished cutting out their felt hearts, have each child tape a heart to the back of someone else's shirt. Be sure everyone is wearing a felt heart.

Have the children get into foursomes, and hand each child a marker and three self-adhesive labels. Say: **Think of at least one good thing about each person in your group. Write that thing on a label, and stick the label to that person's felt heart. Don't stop until everyone is wearing a label from each person in your group.**

After the children have finished, invite them to sit in a circle on the floor. Have them remove the soft hearts from their neighbors' backs. Give each child time to read his or her labels. Then ask:

■ **Do any of the things written on these labels surprise you? Why?**

■ **Describe what it's like to receive this kind of encouragement from others.**

■ **What does the way you feel now tell you about the importance of encouraging others?**

Say: **Taking the time to encourage others can keep them from turning away from God and from giving in to sin. Please take your felt hearts home and put them where you'll see them often. Let them remind you of just how important it is to encourage others.**

HEBREWS
4:12

THEME:
The Bible is always true.

SUMMARY:
Use this SKIT to show children that the answers to many of their questions are in the Bible.

Q & A

SCENE: Children are asking and answering questions.

PROPS: You'll need four Bibles and a table.

CHARACTERS:
You'll need six readers. Three will be Bible Readers and will stand on one side of the stage holding their Bibles. The other three will be Questioners and will stand on the opposite side of the stage without Bibles. You'll also need a child with a Bible to begin the play.

SCRIPT

Child: *(Enters stage holding a Bible. Scoffs and sets the Bible on a table in the middle of the stage.)* The Bible isn't good for anything these days. It's just a bunch of stories about stuff that happened a long time ago. *(Exits.)*

Questioner 1: My parents are so busy with work and their friends. Sometimes I wonder—does anyone really love me?

Bible Reader 1: John 3:16 assures us that "God loved the world so much that he gave his one and only Son so that whoever believes in him may not be lost, but have eternal life."

Questioner 2: I just heard about a little girl who was kidnapped. What can I do when I feel afraid?

Bible Reader 2: Psalm 121:3-8 reminds us that "[The Lord] will not let you be defeated. He who guards you never sleeps. He who guards Israel never rests or sleeps. The Lord guards you. The Lord is the shade that protects you from the sun. The sun cannot hurt you during the day, and the moon cannot hurt you at night. The Lord will protect you from all dangers; he will guard your life. The Lord will guard you as you come and go, both now and forever."

Questioner 3: I keep hearing about things like pollution, crime, gangs, and violence. If God is so good, why are so many bad things happening in the world?

Bible Reader 3: Romans 5:12 explains, "Sin came into the world because of what one man did, and with sin came death. This is why everyone must die—because everyone sinned." But Romans 6:10 adds, "Yes, when Christ died, he died to defeat the power of sin one time—enough for all time. He now has a new life, and his new life is with God."

Questioner 1: The world seems like it's turned away from God. But I'm just a kid; how can I make a difference in my world today?

Bible Reader 1: 1 Timothy 4:12 tells us, "Do not let anyone treat you as if you are unimportant because you are young. Instead, be an example to the believers with your words, your actions, your love, your faith, and your pure life."

Questioner 2: Today was the second day I sat by myself at lunch. I'm so lonely! Isn't there anyone who can be my friend?

Bible Reader 2: Psalm 139 reminds us that God knows us better than anyone else. In fact, verses 7-10 say, "Where can I go to get away from your Spirit? Where can I run from you? If I go up to the heavens, you are there. If I lie down in the grave, you are there. If I rise with the sun in the east and settle in the west beyond the sea, even there you would guide me. With your right hand you would hold me."

Questioner 3: I'm not good at anything! Why did God make me like this?

Bible Reader 3: Genesis 1:27 encourages us by saying, "So God created human beings in his image. In the image of God he created them." And Psalm 8:4-6 adds, "Why are people important to you? Why do you take care of human beings? You made them a little lower than the angels and crowned them with glory and honor. You put them in charge of everything you made. You put all things under their control."

Child: *(Returns to the table and holds up the Bible.)* God's Word is true. The answers are all in the Bible, and God's Word is alive and at work today!

If you use this skit as a discussion starter, here are possible questions:

■ How is the Bible "alive and working" in your life today?

■ What answers have you found in the Bible?

■ Why can the Bible answer our questions today even though it was written so long ago?

■ How can you find your answers in the Bible?

HEBREWS 4:13

THEME:
God knows us inside and out.

SUMMARY:
Use this OBJECT LESSON to help children understand that even their innermost thoughts and feelings are seen by God.

PREPARATION: You'll need a Bible, aluminum foil, wrapping paper, bows, tape, two boxes, and a bag of individually wrapped hard candies. You'll also need "garbage" such as fruit peels and coffee grounds.

Before class, wrap the fruit peels and coffee grounds in foil, then place them in a box. Wrap the box with colorful gift wrap, and add bows. Place the candies in the other box, and tape the box closed. Scribble all over the box, and peel bits of the paper from the sides and top to make the box appear unattractive.

Show the boxes to the class. Say: **There are two mystery boxes here. They're mysteries because you don't know what's inside them. You can touch them, shake them, feel how heavy they are, even sniff them if you'd like. But you can't open them.**

Pass around the containers. Hold the unattractive box up. Then ask:

■ **How many of you would like to have what's inside this box?**

Hold the gift-wrapped box up, then ask:

■ **How many of you would like to have what's inside this box?**

■ **Can you tell just by looking at the boxes what might be inside? Why not?**

Say: **It's impossible to know whether what's inside these boxes is good or bad. We can't see inside them, so we can't judge whether they're good or bad. This is a lot like people. We can't see inside them to know what they're like—but God can! Let's see what the Bible tells us about God seeing inside us.**

Read aloud Hebrews 4:13. Then ask:

■ **What does God know about us?**

■ **Is there anything we can hide from God? our feelings?**

our thoughts? our dreams? our anger?

Say: **God knows exactly what's in our hearts and minds, and we can't hide from him.** If we're thinking bad about someone on the inside but being sweet on the outside, **God knows it.** And if we say we didn't break a pitcher but we really did, **God knows that, too. God sees everything inside us!** Hold up the boxes. Say: **God can even see what's inside these boxes. Let's open them so we can see what's inside, too.**

Let children open the two boxes and see the contents of each. Ask:

■ **Are you surprised at what was inside? Why?**

Say: **Sometimes the prettiest wrappers have the worst gifts inside—just like sometimes people with the nicest smiles are sometimes the meanest inside. But God knows their hearts.**

Hand a hard candy to each child. Invite the children to unwrap the candies and enjoy them as they think about what God might see when he looks inside their hearts. Then close with a prayer. Pray: **Dear God, help us always remember that you know everything about** us—all our thoughts and feelings and everything we do and say. Help us also remember that you hold us responsible for what's inside us. Let this candy remind us to fill ourselves with truly good things rather than with bad thoughts. In Jesus' name, amen.

HEBREWS 7:24-27

THEME:
Jesus helps us approach God.

SUMMARY:
Use this active DEVOTION to help older children discover how Christ intercedes for them.

PREPARATION: You'll need a Bible, tape, a sign that says "God," a paper grocery bag, and a picture of a cross. You'll also need a heavy stone or brick for each child in class.

Before class, tape the sign that says "God" on it at one end of the room. Tape the picture of the cross to a chair, and place the chair a few

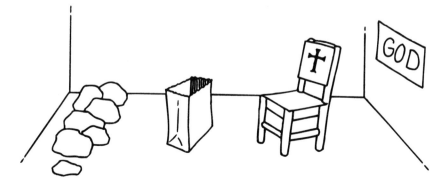

feet in front of the "God" sign. Pile the heavy stones or bricks at the opposite end of the room from the cross. Open the grocery bag, and stand it on the floor between the pile of rocks and the cross.

Have children count off by threes. Ask each group to stand in one area of the room, all about equally distant from the pile of rocks. Say: **Sometimes when we want to feel closer to God, we find that it's not that easy. It's as if something is standing in the way—something we've done or said or thought that we know God wouldn't like. That something turns out to be a big, heavy burden—just like these heavy stones. Think of something you might have done recently or in the past that you know you shouldn't have done—something that probably made God unhappy. Let's hop to the stones, each pick one up, then place the stones in the paper bag.**

When all of the stones are in the paper bag, say: **All these heavy burdens must be carried to God. Let's have someone try to carry the bag of burdens to the God sign across the room.**

Choose one or two children to try lifting the bag. It will either tear or not be moveable. Then say: **It looks like we need a little help.**

Invite children to pile the stones on the chair with the cross, then scoot the chair to the sign. When the "burdens" are delivered, ask:

■ **What made it easier to carry our burdens?**

■ **Can Jesus really carry our**

troubles and burdens? Explain.

■ **How was laying our rocks near the cross like what we need to do when sins stand in the way of getting closer to God?**

Have a volunteer read aloud Hebrews 7:24-27. Then say: **When Jesus gave his life on the cross, he became a sort of "bridge" between God and us. If we give our sins to Jesus, he'll carry them to God for us. Then we're not burdened by sin any longer, and we can draw closer to God.**

Close with this prayer: **We thank you, Jesus, for being like a bridge to God and carrying our burdens. In your name, amen.**

HEBREWS
11:1-12, 17-30

THEME:
We can put our faith in God.

SUMMARY:
This QUIET REFLECTION challenges children to let faith in God replace fear, doubt, and worry.

PREPARATION: You'll need a Bible and small containers of water and sand for each child.

Before class, prepare either a sand container or water container for each child. Baby food jars work well for this activity. You'll need a container for each child in class, but prepare half of the containers with water and the other half with sand.

Have the children sit in a circle. Place the containers of water and sand in the center. Ask:

∎ Did you ever have to do something that was really hard to do?

∎ Did you believe that you could do it? Or were you so afraid you couldn't do it that you didn't even try?

Say: Having faith means being sure of something. The Bible is full of stories about men, women, and children who had faith. Let's read what the Bible says about faith.

Have volunteers read aloud Hebrews 11:1-12, 17-30. Then ask:

∎ What made Abraham obey God's call?

∎ What made Noah believe a flood was coming?

Say: It was faith! Faith made it possible for Noah and Abraham to overcome their fears, doubts, and worries and do what God wanted them to do.

Hold up a container of water. Say: This water reminds us of Noah. Because of Noah's faith in God, God helped Noah save his family and the animals from the worst flood ever to hit the earth. People laughed at Noah because there wasn't even a sign of rain at the time, but Noah didn't let that stop him. He just hammered away. That's some kind of faith!

Hold up a container of sand. Say: The sand reminds us of Abraham. Abraham's faith in God made it possible for him to become the father of as many people as there are grains of sand on a beach. That's some kind of faith, too!

Help yourself to a container of water or a container of sand. Then find a place in the room to think about your own faith in God. Pray for the kind of faith that will make it possible for you to overcome any fears, doubts, or worries you may have about doing whatever God asks you to do. When you leave today, you may take the water or sand home with you. Put it in a place where you can see it the first thing each morning. It'll help chase away your fears, doubts, and worries!

HEBREWS
12:1-3

THEME:
God wants us to persevere through hard times.

SUMMARY:
Use this LEARNING GAME to challenge children to nurture a Christian lifestyle even when it's difficult.

PREPARATION: You'll need a Bible, several small boxes, markers, masking tape, newspaper, and crepe paper.

Before class, mark a "race track" by taping a three-foot wide path through your room. Tape a crepe paper finish line between two chairs at one end of the track. Set the small boxes along the track as hurdles, and scatter newspaper wads along the track.

Have volunteers read aloud Hebrews 12:1-3. Then say: **This Bible passage tells us that living the Christian life is like running a race.** Ask:

■ **What are some things that can keep us from living as Christians and "running" that race well?**

Write on the box hurdles the things that the children mention. Encourage them to name things such as temptation, dishonesty, gossip, and rudeness. Then say: **Sometimes getting rid of the things that hold us back means overcoming them—sort of like jumping over hurdles. And sometimes it means just staying away or dodging them. Now let's have some real fun.**

Today is race day, and this is the Christian Life Racetrack. This is not going to be an easy race. First of all, there are those hurdles to jump over. Then there's all this trash! It stands for all the other things that can interfere with living the Christian life. We need a Runner. Choose one child to be the first Runner, but assure the others that they'll have a turn. Say: **This Runner is going to hop and jump all over the track to dodge obstacles. We'll be members of the Faith Team, and our job is to cheer the Runner on.**

Start each runner by saying "go!" After everyone has run the race and cheered others, read Hebrews 12:1-3 again. Then ask:

■ **How did it feel trying to run this race with all those hurdles to cross and all that trash to dodge?**

■ **How did the Faith Team help you?**

■ **How can faith help us live as Christians?**

Close with this prayer: **Dear God, help us never give up on trying to live the Christian life, no matter how many obstacles we have to deal with. Help us to help others live the Christian life whenever we can. Amen.**

JAMES

"But if any of you needs wisdom, you should ask God for it. He is generous and enjoys giving it to all people, so he will give you wisdom."

James 1:5

JAMES 1:19-20

THEME:

Think before you speak or act out of anger.

SUMMARY:

Use this OBJECT LESSON to demonstrate that being quick to anger can be destructive.

PREPARATION: You'll need a Bible, a can of pop for each child, and damp paper towels. This activity must be done outside in a grassy area.

Have children form pairs, and have partners decide which person in each pair will be "It." Distribute cans of pop, and have children shake their cans of pop while they think of things that make them angry.

Say: **All the Its may point their pop cans away from everyone else and open their cans immediately. Everyone else, wait to open your cans.** After the Its open their cans, ask:

■ **What happened when you opened your can of pop?**

■ **What happens when you're angry and you don't think before you speak or act?**

Pass out damp paper towels, and let the children wipe up any pop that sprayed on them. Have the children slowly count to ten with you; then let the rest of the children open their pop cans. Ask:

■ **What happened when you**

waited to open your can of pop?

■ **How is that like waiting to speak when someone makes you mad?**

Have a volunteer read James 1:19-20. Ask:

■ **What are James' suggestions about what to do when anger bubbles up?**

■ **How can you stop and think before you speak or act when you're angry?**

Lead the children in praying: **Dear God, sometimes anger bubbles up inside us so fast that we explode, blurting out hurtful words or doing mean things. Help us to be slow to anger and to think before we act. Amen.**

Let the children drink their pops after the prayer.

JAMES
2:1-4

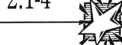

THEME:
Love your neighbor as you love yourself.

SUMMARY:
Use this AFFIRMATION ACTIVITY to help children see the joy that comes from encouraging each other.

PREPARATION: You'll need a Bible, a pencil, slips of paper, and uninflated balloons. You'll also need a cassette player and a cassette of upbeat music.

Before this activity, write different encouraging acts on slips of paper. You might include affirmations such as "Give three people a high five," "Tell two friends why you're glad they're here," and "Gather everyone in a group hug." You'll need one slip of paper for each child in your class. Roll up the slips and place each one inside an uninflated balloon. Blow up the balloons and tie them off.

Have children sit in a circle. Turn on the cassette player, bop one balloon into the circle, and have children pass the balloon to their right. After a few seconds, stop the cassette player and say: (Name of child holding the balloon), **find a fun way to pop the balloon, then read and follow the instructions inside.** The child may pop the balloon by sitting on it, stepping on it, using the point of a pencil, or squishing the balloon against a wall.

After the first child has followed the instructions inside the balloon, start the music again, and bop another balloon into the circle. Continue until each child has a chance to pop a balloon and affirm others. Then have a volunteer read James 2:1-4. Ask:

■ **What was it like to be treated with kindness?**

■ **Why does God want us to love everyone around us?**

■ **When is it hard to love people around you?**

Say: **In our game, you had to get past the balloon to find a fun way to encourage your friends. In real life, God wants us to get past what people look like and find new ways to love them.**

JAMES
2:14-17

THEME:
God wants us to act out our faith.

SUMMARY:
On this field TRIP, children discover what it means to actually feed the hungry or clothe the poor.

PREPARATION: You'll need a Bible and a signed permission slip for each child.

Contact a local food kitchen or homeless shelter, and arrange for your group to volunteer for a few hours. Children can stock shelves with canned and dry goods, greet people at the door, help set up tables, or serve food. It's important that children have an opportunity to participate in the actual hands-on service instead of just watching others serve.

Afterward, gather everyone together. Ask:

■ **Describe how you felt when you first saw the people who come to the shelter for help?**

■ **How did it feel to serve those people?**

Have a volunteer read James 2:14-17. Ask:

■ **What's the difference between just saying something and actually doing it?**

■ **What other ways can we act out our faith?**

JAMES
4:7-8

THEME:
When we stand against the devil, he runs away.

SUMMARY:
In this OBJECT LESSON, children discover God's power against Satan.

PREPARATION: You'll need a Bible, water, paper cups, small containers of black pepper, and containers of dishwashing liquid.

Have children form pairs, and give each pair a cup of water, a small container of black pepper, and a container of dishwashing liquid.

Say: **Take turns shaking pepper onto the surface of the water in your cups. As you shake the pepper, tell your partner the wrong things that Satan wants us to do—lie, steal, disobey our parents, and swear, for example.**

After a few seconds, have children stop shaking the pepper. Ask:

■ **How does the water look?**

Read James 4:7-8 aloud then say: **When we pray, we're calling on God's power. The power of God is strong enough to take all the sin out of our hearts and send Satan running. Pray with your partner, and ask God to forgive you for the bad things you've done.**

After the children have prayed, say: **Now take the dishwashing liquid and add one tiny drop to your cups.** Pause for children to

follow your instructions. Ask:
■ **What happened to the pepper?**
■ **How is that like what happens to sin when we pray?**
Say: **Just as the pepper "ran away" when you added soap, Satan runs away when we pray. Prayer is powerful!**

JAMES 4:13-17

THEME:
God doesn't want us to brag.

SUMMARY:
Use this SKIT to help children realize that bragging is wrong.

BRAGGERS ANONYMOUS

SCENE: Several people are attending a "Braggers Anonymous" meeting.

PROPS: You'll need several chairs, a spray bottle filled with water, loaded squirt guns, a gavel or small wooden hammer, and a podium or small desk.

CHARACTERS:
Kaitlin (an older girl)
Matt (any age boy)
Mia (any age girl, dressed nicely)
Derek (any age boy)
Children (at least five children to fill in the meeting)

SCRIPT
(Chairs are arranged in a circle. Characters are milling around, talking. Kaitlin steps to the podium and pounds the gavel.)

Kaitlin: Members! Members! It's time to start our meeting, so I need everyone to take a seat. *(When members are seated, Kaitlin continues.)*

Kaitlin: Welcome to tonight's meeting of Braggers Anonymous. We're all here because each of us has a problem with bragging or boasting about things we've done or are going to do. Let's start our meeting by reciting the group's motto.

Everyone: Listening to someone boast and brag isn't just wrong—it's really a drag.

Kaitlin: Wonderful! For all our new members, my name's Kaitlin, and I'll be leading our meeting tonight. This evening, we'll be trying a new method to break the bragging cycle. *(Pulls out the spray bottle.)* As you're telling us about what you did this week, I'll be listening for anything that sounds like bragging. If you forget and start to brag, I'll give you a little squirt to remind you that bragging is wrong. Ready? Who'd like to start?

(Several characters raise their hands.)

Kaitlin: How about Matt?

Matt: *(Stands up nervously.)* Well, I...uh...had a good week. My family and I went to...um... uh...Disneyland. Yeah, that's it. *(Gaining confidence)* And we rode on all the rides...two... three...four times! And my dad bought me two hundred dollars worth of—

(Kaitlin interrupts him with a squirt from the spray bottle.)

Matt: Hey, watch it!

Kaitlin: Matt, you were starting to brag about your trip.

(Matt sits down.)

Kaitlin: Let's see if someone else wants to share. *(Hands raise.)* Mia?

Mia: *(Snobbishly)* Well, let's see. Monday I went shopping and bought a whole new wardrobe for school. Then Tuesday I went shopping and bought the biggest, best Barbie bed. And on Wednesday, Scott Taylor said I was the prettiest—

(Kaitlin interrupts Mia with a squirt from the spray bottle.)

Mia: Oh, you'll ruin my new clothes!

Kaitlin: Mia, you were bragging big time! No one wants to hear about all the expensive things you bought. It's rude!

(Mia sits down.)

Kaitlin: Hmm, would anyone else like to share without bragging? Derek?

Derek: *(Looking anxiously at the spray bottle)* OK, let's see. Um, my week was all right. I studied really hard all week and got the highest grade in class on my science test. *(Kaitlin picks up the spray bottle.)* But it was just because I studied so hard. Then at soccer practice I scored two goals ... *(hurriedly, as if covering his tracks)* with the help of my teammates. I couldn't have done it without them!

Kaitlin: Wonderful, Derek! I think you're starting to understand what we mean by not bragging or boasting. *(Derek sits down. Kaitlin moves to the middle of the circle as she begins her speech.)* And that's just why I started this club. I'm great at organizing things, and since I started this club, I've led several—I mean *hundreds* of meetings and have changed the lives of *(pause)* millions of people. I'm so talented and great that one day I'll be the world's most popular leader. Maybe I'll even have my own talk show! And then, I'll—

(Group members pull out water guns and squirt Kaitlin.)

Kaitlin: Aargh! *(Kaitlin runs offstage.)*

Permission to photocopy this skit from *The Children's Worker's Encyclopedia of Bible-Teaching Ideas: NT* granted for local church use. Copyright © Group Publishing, Inc., P.O. Box 481, Loveland, CO 80539.

If you use this skit as a discussion starter, here are possible questions:

■ **What things do people brag about?**

■ **Why is it wrong to boast and brag?**

■ **What do you feel like when you hear someone brag?**

■ **What are other things you can say when you're tempted to brag?**

1 PETER

"You have not seen Christ, but still you love him. You cannot see him now, but you believe in him. So you are filled with a joy that cannot be explained, a joy full of glory."

1 Peter 1:8

1 PETER 1:6-9

THEME:
We can face life's obstacles because we know Jesus loves us and died for us.

SUMMARY:
In this LEARNING GAME, children navigate an obstacle course to reach a reward.

PREPARATION: You'll need a Bible and cookies or doughnuts.

Before this activity, set up a simple obstacle course outside. You might include a slide, sawhorses, or tires for children to run through.

Gather children outside, and show them how to run through the obstacle course. Say: **We'll take turns going through this obstacle course of "troubles." At the end, you'll each receive a tasty prize!** After each child has finished the obstacle course, distribute the snack. As children eat, ask:

■ **What was the hardest part of the obstacle course?**

■ **What kept you going when the course was difficult?**

Have a volunteer read 1 Peter 1:6-9. Ask:

■ **What troubles do we face in real life?**

■ **What good things come from hard times?**

■ **What can we look forward to when we're going through**

hard times?

Say: **When the obstacle course was difficult, you kept going because you knew a terrific prize was waiting for you. When life gets hard, we can keep going because we know that Jesus loves us and died for our sins. We know we've got a wonderful home waiting for us in heaven.**

1 PETER
2:1

THEME:
Sin makes us unclean.

SUMMARY:
Use this SKIT to help children discover how sin accumulates in our lives and makes us "dirty."

SPIC AND SPAN

SCENE: A boy is cleaning his room.

PROPS: You'll need a table, a large box, and poster board signs that read "evil," "lying," "hypocrisy," "jealousy," and "evil speech." The signs should be smudged and should have wet paint, mud, or grease stuck to them.

CHARACTER:
Boy (elementary age, wearing a plain white T-shirt and jeans that can get dirty)

SCRIPT
(Boy enters carrying the cardboard box filled with "dirty signs." He looks annoyed.)
Boy: I can't believe my mom is making me clean out my box of favorite stuff! She doesn't understand that I need these things. *(Sighs.)* Well, let me see if there's anything here I can possibly part with. *(Pulls out the "evil" sign and smiles.)* Evil! Just thinking of all the cool stuff we've done together makes me smile. *(Holds sign close to him as he talks, getting himself dirty.)* Like making Jennifer Murphy pay me her lunch money for three weeks. Or the time I threw rocks at old Mr. Gardner's house on Halloween night. *(Looks at sign.)* I can't get rid of evil! Hmm, maybe I can hide it. *(Stuffs the sign under his shirt.)* There—Mom will never find it now.

Well, what else is in here? *(Pulls out the "lying" sign.)* Lying! Oh, the memories this brings back. *(Hugs sign to his cheek, getting his face dirty.)* Making up stories about why I didn't do my homework, inventing juicy gossip about other kids at school, telling whoppers about my summer vacation—lying is so fun! I can't get rid of this! But where can I hide it? Let's see, if I put it under my bed, Mom won't find it. *(Puts sign under the table and giggles.)* I'll just lie and tell her I threw it away!

OK, so far so good. *(Pulls the "hypocrisy" sign from the box.)* Ah, my old friend hypocrisy. Bragging about how I go to church when I really go to make fun of the other kids. Telling people what a good Christian I am even though I love to lie, steal, and cheat. Letting people know how wonderful I am even though this box is full of stuff I shouldn't have. *(Kisses the sign, getting dirt on his face.)* I couldn't bear to part with my hypocrisy! So I think I'll just roll up the sign and stick it in my back pocket. *(Rolls up the sign and shoves it into a pocket.)* That's better.

Well, what do we have left? *(Pulls out the "jealousy" sign.)* All right—jealousy! I haven't seen this good friend since Christmas. That's when I was so jealous of Trevor's new pro-style football that I popped it! Oh, and when I was jealous of Bobby's good grades, I made up a story that he'd cheated. Where can I hide jealousy? Maybe there's room alongside evil. *(Tucks sign under shirt.)*

Only one thing left in my box—evil speech. *(Pulls out the "evil speech" sign.)* Boy, does this come in handy when you want to talk about someone. Or when you're really mad at your parents. Or when you want to make someone cry. Yeah, I sure need this. So I'll just tuck it up under my pant leg, like so. *(Pushes sign up pant leg.)*

There! *(Turns box upside down.)* Mom should be happy that I've cleaned up. *(Looks at dirty shirt, arms, and pants.)* Well, I've sort of cleaned up. *(Takes box off-stage.)*

Permission to photocopy this skit from *The Children's Worker's Encyclopedia of Bible-Teaching Ideas: NT* granted for local church use. Copyright © Group Publishing, Inc., P.O. Box 481, Loveland, CO 80539.

If you use this skit as a discussion starter, here are possible questions:

■ How do things like lying, evil speech, and hypocrisy make us dirty?

■ Why do we let things like lying and jealousy stay in our lives?

■ Why does God want us to get rid of those things?

■ What qualities should we hold onto?

■ Who can cleanse us of our sins?

1 PETER
3:13-18

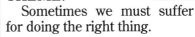

THEME:
Sometimes we must suffer for doing the right thing.

SUMMARY:
In this active DEVOTION, children explore what it feels like to suffer for doing right.

PREPARATION: You'll need a Bible and newspaper.

EXPERIENCE
Have children form two groups, and have the groups gather at opposite ends of the room. Set a pile of newspapers near Group 2. Huddle with Group 1 and say: **You're the Do-Rights. Follow my instructions.** Huddle with Group 2 and tell them: **You're the Wrongdoers. When we start the activity, ignore what I say. When I tell the class to stand, remain seated. When I tell them to march around the classroom, crumple up these sheets of newspaper and make**

balls. When I tell them to sit in a circle, point at them and say, "You bunch of Do-Rights" and throw the paper balls at them.

To the entire class, say: **Everyone stand up.** (The Do-Rights will be the only ones to stand.) **March around the room five times.** (The Wrongdoers will make paper balls while the others march.) **Sit in a circle on the floor.** (Signal the Wrongdoers to throw the paper balls.) **Now our activity is over.**

Have the groups switch roles to repeat the activity.

RESPONSE

Ask :

■ **How did you feel when the Wrongdoers threw things at you?**

■ **Do you think it's fair that the Wrongdoers didn't have to follow my instructions? Why or why not?**

■ **What was it like to follow instructions that others ignored?**

■ **What was it like to ignore my instructions?**

■ **Do you think it's fair that the Wrongdoers didn't have the same instructions as the Do-Rights? Why or why not?**

Read 1 Peter 3:13-18. Ask:

■ **What does this passage tell us about doing right?**

■ **Why is it OK to suffer for obeying God?**

CLOSING

Say: **Some people may not like it when you follow God. They may tease you or make fun of you. But the Bible says that we don't have to fear people like that. Jesus died for them, too. Instead of getting** angry or hurt, we can pray for people who don't know or love Jesus. Let's pray right now.

Have children say simple one-sentence prayers for friends who don't know Jesus.

1 PETER
4:10-11

THEME:

We can use our talents for God.

SUMMARY:

With this SERVICE PROJECT, children discover that everyone has a special gift to share with others.

PREPARATION: Before this activity, contact a nursing home and arrange for your group to put on a talent show for the residents.

Have a volunteer read 1 Peter 4:10-11.

Say: **Each person here has a special talent or gift he or she can use for God. Let's use our talents to encourage the residents of a nursing home.**

Encourage the children to consider talents such as singing, reading a story or a poem, ballet or tap dancing, clowning, leading a sing-along, or playing an instrument. Children can form groups to perform a skit, put on a puppet show, or sing songs. Children who don't want to perform may design scenery for a skit, be in charge of props, or assist the other children as a stage manager. Remind children that each person is special and has many gifts to contribute.

1 PETER
5:7

THEME:
God cares for us.

SUMMARY:
Use this creative PRAYER to teach children to bring their worries to God.

PREPARATION: You'll need a Bible, one-by-six-inch paper strips, pens, and tape.

Give each child a pen and six paper strips. Tell children to write one of the following concerns on each strip:

1. a person you're worried about,

2. something you're worried about at home,

3. something you're worried about at school,

4. a future event you're worried about,

5. something in your community that frightens you, and

6. something in our world that frightens you.

Show children how to tape the ends of one strip together to form a ring, then slide another strip through the ring and tape the ends together. Have children continue making their "worries" into paper chains, using all six of the paper strips.

Have children form a circle, and instruct them to wrap their chains around their waists. Say: **Our worries can chain us up with feelings of fear and frustration. But 1 Peter 5:7 says, "Give all your worries to him because he cares about you." Let's pray and give our worries to God. As I read each part of the prayer, tear that worry from your chain and toss it into the middle of the circle. You may keep the remainder of your chain to remind you of how God frees us from worries.**

Read the following prayer, pausing after each phrase:

Dear God, we worry about so many things.

Like friends and family members,

Situations at home,

Things at school,

Events that might happen in the future,

Scary things in our neighborhoods,

And frightening events in our world.

Help us turn to you and give all our cares to you as we remember how much you love us. I know you care for me, and no worry is too large or too small to bring to you in prayer. Amen.

2 PETER

"But God is being patient with you. He does not want anyone to be lost, but he wants all people to change their hearts and lives."

2 Peter 3:9b

---

2 PETER
1:5-8

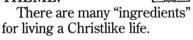

THEME:
There are many "ingredients" for living a Christlike life.

SUMMARY:
Use this food CRAFT to teach children the character traits God wants us to have.

PREPARATION: Have each child bring one of the following food items: one cup of maraschino cherries, one cup of pineapple chunks, one cup of shredded coconut, one cup of miniature marshmallows, one cup of mandarin orange wedges, and one cup of plain or vanilla yogurt. You'll also need a

Bible, index cards, a large bowl, a large spoon, and a paper bowl and a spoon for each child.

Before class, write each of the character traits from 2 Peter 1:5-8 on a separate index card. As children arrive, have them place the food items on a table. Tape a character-trait card to the front of each food container.

Have children gather around the table. Say: **Each of these foods is an important part of the recipe for a tasty snack.** Have a volunteer read 2 Peter 1:5-8. Say: **This verse tells us the recipe for a Christlike life. Let's mix them together and see what we get.**

Place a large bowl on the table. Then ask another volunteer to read the Scripture again, pausing after each character trait. As each trait is mentioned, ask a different child to find the food item with that label and pour the item into the large bowl. When each ingredient has been added, stir them together. Put about three spoonfuls in a paper bowl for each child, and allow children to enjoy the tasty treat. As children eat, talk about how we can demonstrate each of the character traits mentioned in the Bible passage.

2 PETER
3:17-18

THEME:
It's important to listen for God's voice.

SUMMARY:
Use this LEARNING GAME to show children how easy it is to be led astray.

PREPARATION: Before this activity, set up a simple obstacle course. You might place chairs or cones around your playing area for children to walk around or set up tables for them to crawl under. You'll also need a Bible and scarves or bandannas.

Have the children form three groups, and give each member of Group 1 a scarf or bandanna. Help children tie the scarves around their heads as blindfolds; then ask members of Group 1 to join hands or link arms.

Have Groups 2 and 3 scatter around the obstacle course. Show children the path through the course, then explain that Group 1 will try to go through the course blindfolded. Group 2 will shout helpful directions, but Group 3 will call out false directions. After Group 1 goes through the course, have groups trade roles and play again. After each group has had a turn going through the obstacle course, form a circle and ask:

■ **What was difficult about going through the obstacle course?**

■ **What would have made it easier?**

Read 2 Peter 3:17-18. Then ask:

■ **What wrong things do some people want you to do?**

■ **How can you keep doing good things instead of following those evil people?**

Say: **Some people will try to get you to steal, lie, cheat, or do other wrong things. They're trying to pull you away from doing right. Just as you listened for the right instructions in our game, it's important to listen for God's voice as we go through life's obstacles.**

1 JOHN

*"But if we confess our sins, he will
forgive our sins, because we can
trust God to do what is right."*

1 John 1:9a

---

1 JOHN
1:8-9

THEME:
If we confess, God forgives
our sins.

SUMMARY:
In this QUIET REFLECTION, children learn that God washes
away our sins.

PREPARATION: Before this activity, smudge several hand mirrors
with dirt. You'll need one mirror
for every two children. You'll also
need a Bible, paper towels, and a
bowl of soapy water.

Have the children form pairs, and
give one smudged mirror to
each pair. Tell children to look into
their mirrors. Say: **Sin can make it
hard to see ourselves clearly. But
God looks at our hearts, and
even if they're smudged with sin,
he still knows us and loves us.**

Read 1 John 1:8-9 aloud. Have
children bow their heads and
silently ask God to forgive them for
the bad things they've done.

Say: **Choose one partner to
bring the mirror to the bowl of
soapy water and wash the mirror.
The other partner will dry the mirror with paper towels.** When pairs
have cleaned their mirrors, have
them look at their reflections again.
Say: **You can be sure that God forgives you when you ask him to. He
cleans the sin from your heart and
wipes the sadness from your eyes.
Look in your mirrors and thank
God for his love and forgiveness.**

1 JOHN
2:12-14

THEME:
We can encourage each other.

SUMMARY:
In this AFFIRMATION ACTIVITY, children encourage each other through letter-writing.

PREPARATION: You'll need a piece of stationery and a pen for each child. You'll also need a Bible.

Read 1 John 2:12-14 aloud. Say: **John wrote to Christians to encourage them and to remind them that Jesus died for their sins. We can encourage each other in letters, too.**

Have children form groups of six or eight. Distribute pens and sheets of decorative stationery. Then tell children to write, "Dear (child's own name), I write to you because..." at the top of their papers. Instruct children to pass their papers around the circle, allowing each person in their group to write positive statements about them. You may want to play a cassette of praise music while children are writing. When the letters come back to the senders, have children read their own letters silently. Then bring the groups together and ask:

■ **What was it like to read the positive things your friends wrote?**

■ **How do you think the early Christians felt when they read what John wrote to them?**

■ **Why is it so important to encourage each other?**

Say: **It feels good to hear people say positive things about us. Remember to encourage and praise others so they can feel good about themselves, too.**

1 JOHN
4:1, 4

THEME:
God wants us to reject people who lie about him.

SUMMARY:
Use this SKIT to teach children to watch out for false teachings.

SOLD OUT

SCENE: A crowd is gathered at a street corner.

PROPS: You'll need a small table and a suitcase filled with Bibles.

CHARACTERS:
Malcolm D. Seever (preferably an older boy, dressed in a hat and cape or coat to look like a "snake oil salesman")
Onlookers (five children of various ages)
Passersby (any number of children to walk by or stop to watch the show)

SCRIPT
(Malcolm enters with his suitcase, noisily sets it on the table, and opens it.)
Malcolm: Step right up, ladies and gentlemen. I, Malcolm D. Seever, have *the* latest, *the* greatest, *the*

most amazing product to come down the pike since Hostess invented Twinkies. *(A crowd gathers.)* Yes, ladies and gentlemen, you won't want to walk away empty-handed when you see what I've brought today! *(Pulls out a Bible.)* The new, improved, modern, and absolutely harmless Bible. *(Crowd begins to disperse, disappointed.)* Now before you walk away, let me remind you that this Bible isn't like any you've read before.

Onlooker 1: *(Scoffing)* Yeah, right—just another book full of rules telling me all the fun stuff I can't do.

Malcolm: *(To Onlooker 1)* Open this Bible, and you won't even find the Ten Commandments. We've changed them to the Ten Suggestions. And sin—why, I challenge you to find that very word in this Bible! *(Onlooker looks interested and picks up a Bible.)* That's right! No mention of sin or its consequences. According to this Bible, you can do whatever you like, as long as it feels good!

Onlooker 2: What about all that jazz about following God? I'll bet your Bible says I have to do *that.*

Malcolm: Wrong again, friends! The new, improved, modern, and absolutely harmless Bible tells you to follow your heart. Whatever you feel like doing... well, that must be the right thing to do. Don't you all agree? *(Some passersby and onlookers nod their heads.)*

Onlooker 3: OK, OK, but I'll bet it tells us to love others. I always hated that part of my Bible. I mean, I'm actually supposed to love my enemies?

Malcolm: I can sympathize with you. Many a night I've wondered how that nonsense made it into the Bible. So we've simply taken it out! You only have to love the people you want to love. And you only have to love them if they love you back! What a deal, folks! Step right up and get your new, improved, modern, and absolutely harmless Bible today!

Onlooker 4: So I don't need to forgive others, either?

Malcolm: Forgiveness? Completely erased from this Bible! You don't have to forgive, love, care about, or even talk to anyone! In fact, you'll read about ways to hold a grudge, get revenge, and give people the cold shoulder like a pro!

Onlooker 5: How 'bout all those verses about worshiping God? What does your Bible have to say about that?

Malcolm: Worship should be reserved for yourself. When you look in the mirror, there's your worship service! No need to go to church, sing about God or Jesus, or... or even pray! You can spend that time telling yourself how special you are! And I, Malcolm D. Seever, will personally guarantee your satisfaction if you purchase one of these Bibles.

(Onlookers and passersby huddle around the table, then leave carrying Bibles. Onlooker 2 is at the back of the crowd and reaches Malcolm after others are gone.)

Onlooker 2: *(Sadly)* Looks like

you sold out, Mr. Seever.

Malcolm: *(Slyly, with a smile)* Not me, friend. *(Pause.)* They sold out.

If you use this skit as a discussion starter, here are possible questions:

■ Why did the people in this skit "buy" a new set of beliefs?

■ Why don't some people in the world want you to believe in the Bible?

■ What lies and false teachings have you heard at school? on TV? from your friends?

■ How can you tell if a teaching or belief goes against the Bible?

2 JOHN

"And now, dear lady, this is not a new command but is the same command we have had from the beginning. I ask you that we all love each other."

2 John 5

2 JOHN
5-6

THEME:
God commands us to walk in love.

SUMMARY:
In this QUIET REFLECTION, children think about what it means to love.

PREPARATION: You'll need a Bible, markers, scissors, and several paper grocery sacks.

Read 2 John 5-6, then say: **God commands us to walk in love.** Ask:
■ **What does it mean to walk in love?**

■ **Why does God want us to do those things?**

Give each child a marker and a paper grocery sack. Tell children to put their feet on the paper and trace around them and then cut out the footprints.

Form groups of no more than five. Say: **On each footprint, write down what you think love is.** When children have finished writing, have each group lay its footprints out to form a trail.

Say: **Take turns walking along your group's trail of love. Read and think about each definition as you step on it.**

After everyone has had a chance to "walk in love," pray: **Dear God, help us use these ideas to show love to each other. Show us how to obey your command to walk in love. Amen.**

3 JOHN

"My dear friend, do not follow what is bad; follow what is good."

3 John 11a

3 JOHN
5-8

THEME:
We can extend hospitality to missionaries.

SUMMARY:
Use this SERVICE PROJECT to raise money for missionaries.

PREPARATION: You'll need a Bible, paper, markers, poster board, and a song book.

Several weeks before your service project, have a volunteer read 3 John 5-8. Explain that missionaries need lots of support so they can tell others about Jesus.

They need supplies such as Bibles, books, and music, and they need money to pay for food, housing, and transportation. Tell children that they can help raise money to help missionaries.

Arrange for children to put on a concert of praise music before a church service or between church and Sunday school. Each week, practice a few of the children's favorite praise songs. Choose about ten short, active songs that most children are familiar with. Have children make posters to advertise the event.

At the concert, distribute a list of the songs children will sing; include a price next to each song. Prices should be no more than five dollars. Explain that adults must donate the listed price to hear each song. You may suggest that several adults put in a few cents to raise the money. Kick off the concert by having a child read 3 John 5-8, and then tell the adults that the money will go to church missionaries.

3 JOHN
11

THEME:
We should follow Jesus.

SUMMARY:
In this MUSIC activity, children will share ways to follow Jesus.

PREPARATION: You'll need a Bible, a cassette player, and a cassette recording of "I Have Decided to Follow Jesus."

Gather children together, then read 3 John 11 aloud. Ask:

■ **Who's the best person to follow?**

■ **How do you show you're following Jesus?**

Say: **Let's learn a song that talks about following Jesus.**

Teach children the words to "I Have Decided to Follow Jesus," then lead them in singing it twice. When children are comfortable with the words, have them form four groups. Have each group come up with a creative way to move around the room in time to the music. Children might take giant steps, walk sideways, or combine backward and forward steps.

Lead children in singing the song again, but have each group take turns leading others around the room in their chosen manner. After children follow the last group, form a circle and ask:

■ **How can we follow Jesus every day?**

■ **How will your life be different when you follow Jesus?**

JUDE

"God is strong and can help you not to fail. He can bring you before his glory without any wrong in you and can give you great joy."

Jude 24

JUDE 17-21

THEME:
Remain strong in your faith even when others doubt God.

SUMMARY:
Use this MUSIC IDEA to help children discover all the fun ways we can keep our faith strong.

PREPARATION: You'll need a Bible, matches, an oil lamp, lamp oil, a cassette player, and a cassette recording of "Give Me Oil in My Lamp."

Before children arrive, fill the oil lamp halfway with lamp oil, and light the wick. Place the lamp in a safe place like a corner table or a high shelf.

Have children sit in a circle. Read Jude 17-21, then ask:
■ **What is your reaction when people laugh about God?**
■ **What goes through your mind when you see people doing bad things?**
Say: **This Bible passage tells us to keep doing good things and believing in Jesus even though people might laugh or do bad things.** Point to the oil lamp. **This lamp will keep burning as long as it has oil in it. When people put down our faith, it's sort of like emptying our "oil supply." It's frustrating, and it can wear us down. But God wants us to remain strong and faithful.**

Teach children the song "Give Me Oil in My Lamp." You might include other fun verses such as "Give me gas for my Ford; keep me truckin' for the Lord" or "Give me hot sauce on my taco; let me witness in Morocco."

During the chorus, have the boys stand for the word "sing" and the girls stand for the word "hosan-na." Children may point to heaven on the word "king." Allow children to make up their own verses to think of ways to keep "burning" for Jesus.

Say: **Whenever you feel frustrated or whenever people put down your faith, just make up a new verse and keep burning!**

REVELATION

"Here I am! I stand at the door and knock.
If you hear my voice and open the door,
I will come in and eat with you, and
you will eat with me."

Revelation 3:20

REVELATION 7:9-12

THEME:
Everyone around the world can praise God.

SUMMARY:
Use this PARTY to help children learn that people of all nations worship and praise God.

PREPARATION: Several weeks before the party, send out invitations that look like flags of different countries. Encourage children to come dressed in simple costumes that represent their heritage—a sash, turban, sombrero, sari, cowboy hat, poncho, or kilt, for example. Ask children to bring a food item that represents their heritage as well, such as tacos, egg rolls, Irish stew, or hamburgers.

Decorate the room with flags or banners from around the world. You might hold a contest to see how many flags children can identify. Play games such as...

■ Name a Country. Have the children stand in a circle. Give one child a ball, and tell him or her to name a country and then toss the ball to someone else. The child who catches the ball must then name a country that begins with the last letter of the previous country—for example, Chile, Ecuador, Rwanda, Argentina, etc. To give children a few ideas, you may want to put posters around the room that display the names of different countries.

■ Letter Game. Have the children form a circle. Begin with the letter "a," and fill in the blanks of the following chant with words that begin with "a":

A: my name is (name that begins with "a").

My husband's (or wife's) **name is** (name that begins with "a").

We live in (country that begins with "a"),

And we sell (any item that begins with "a").

An example is: "A: My name is Agatha. My husband's name is Arnold. We live in Africa, and we sell ants."

The child to your right will do the rhyme with the letter "b," and others will continue through the alphabet.

Before children eat, lead them in praying for the people of different nations. Children may pray for the countries they represent or may choose a country that interests them.

REVELATION 8:3-4

THEME:
God hears our prayers.

SUMMARY:
Use this creative PRAYER to help children imagine their prayers rising to God.

PREPARATION: You'll need a Bible, matches, and an incense stick or cone for each child. If incense is difficult to find, you may use votive candles.

Have children form a circle, and distribute the incense sticks or candles. Read Revelation 8:3-4. Say: **In biblical times, people often burned incense while they prayed. We can imagine our prayers rising like a pleasant aroma to God.**

Go around the circle and light each child's incense stick. Have children say simple, one-sentence prayers of thanks or praise to God. Children might say things such as "Thank you, God, for my parents," or "God, you're awesome."

When all the incense sticks are lit, lead children in praying: **Dear God, thank you for hearing all of our prayers. May our prayers be like a sweet perfume that we offer to you. In Jesus' name, amen.**

REVELATION 21:1-4

THEME:
There won't be any sadness in heaven.

SUMMARY:
Use this SKIT to help children understand the joy that awaits them in heaven.

BORDER PATROL

SCENE: New groups are arriving at heaven's gate.

PROPS: You'll need a clipboard; two chairs; a large box; and one heavy item for each child, such as a brick, a large book, or a box.

Before the skit, have each child in the skit choose a reason for sadness, such as pain, death, hunger, failure, loneliness, fear, or worry. Instruct the children to keep their reasons for sadness a secret until it's time to share them in the skit. Have the children stand at one end of the room. Direct Gabby to stand in the middle of the room near a large box and two chairs which are set up as heaven's gate. The children or groups of children will go to the gate one at a time.

CHARACTERS:
Gabby (dressed completely in white and holding a clipboard)
Children (four children or small groups of children, each holding a heavy object)

SCRIPT
(Gabby is doodling on her clipboard as the first group of Children approach.)
Gabby: *(Singing in any tune)* Heaven's gate is where I wait, so don't be late or hesitate. It's really great; let's make a date… *(Notices first group of Children standing before her.)* Oh, hi. Welcome to heaven. I'm Gabby, and I'm here to check to see if you're carrying any sadness, sorrow, or pain. Do you have any of those things?
(Children in the first group nod and say they are carrying sadness.)
Gabby: Why are you sad today?
(Children tell their reasons.)
Gabby: OK, I'm glad to say you'll be leaving those things here. *(Motions to the large box.)* There's the drop-off point; just drop your burdens and go on inside.
(Children in the first group drop their heavy items in the box.

Gabby pretends to check off the items as Children file through.)
Gabby: Okey-doke…let's see… where was I? Oh yeah. *(Begins singing again)* If you're sad, now be glad 'cuz heaven's rad; it's not a fad… (Notices second group of Children standing before her.)* Oh, hi. Just singin' along here. *(Clears throat and becomes "official.")* Are you carrying any sorrow, sadness, or pain?
(Children in the second group nod.)
Gabby: And what heavy burdens are you carrying today?
(Children tell their reasons for sadness.)
Gabby: Alrighty then, it's time to relieve you of your burdens for eternity. *(Motions to box.)* Just drop them in the box as you file through, and enjoy your eternal life in heaven. *(Pretends to check off the heavy items as Children drop them in the box, then begins singing again)* Ohh, heaven's aglow, so don't be slow. You've got to go or do-si-do, so don't say no… *(Notices third group of Children standing before her.)* Wow, it's sure a busy day! Good morning, folks, and welcome to the pearly gates. Are you carrying any heavy burdens today?
(Children in third group nod.)
Gabby: And what are the causes of your burdens?
(Children in group three tell the reasons for their pain.)
Gabby: Fortunately we don't allow any sadness, sorrow, or pain inside God's kingdom. So if you have any of those heavy things, I'll have to ask you to leave them here. *(Motions to the box.)* Then just file through the gates, follow that street of gold, and eternal

life is yours! *(Pretends to check items off as children drop them in the box, then wipes her forehead.)* My, this gate job is a lot of work! *(Looks in box.)* I never realized that people carry so much pain and suffering with them. What a heavy load! *(Resumes singing)* But not in here—no pain or tears. Just leave your fears. It's crystal clear, and God is near... *(Notices fourth group of Children standing before her. Sighs and points to the box.)* Here's the box, what's your burden?

(Children in fourth group tell Gabby their reasons for sadness.)

Gabby: I've got good news and better news. The good news is that you have to leave your sadness, sorrow, and pain here. The better news is that you get to spend eternity in heaven with God! He's prepared a place for each of you just inside these gates. So if you'll drop your burdens in the box, you can start enjoying heaven right away! *(Pretends to check items off as children file through; then she looks around to see if anyone is watching, drops her clipboard in the box, and dances through the gates.)*

If you use this skit as a discussion starter, here are possible questions:

■ **What heavy burdens will you be glad to leave behind?**

■ **Why can't there be sadness or pain in heaven?**

■ **What do you think heaven will be like?**

REVELATION 22:1-5

THEME:
Heaven is a wonderful place.

SUMMARY:
On this field TRIP, children share their ideas about heaven and learn the Bible's description of heaven.

PREPARATION: You'll need paper, pens, a Bible, and apples or some other fruit.

Be sure to obtain written permission from each child's parent or caregiver to participate. Also, you may want to recruit extra drivers or volunteers.

Take a trip to a lake, stream, creek, or fountain. Give the children a few minutes to explore the water, observe it, feel it, and listen to it. Gather with the children near the water, distribute paper and pens, then give children five minutes to write down what they think heaven will be like.

Collect the papers, shuffle them, and pass them out again. Let each child read aloud the description on his or her piece of paper. Read Revelation 22:1-5, then ask:

■ **How does the Bible's description of heaven sound to you?**

■ **What do you like best about it? Why?**

■ **How does it compare to some of the descriptions we heard today?**

Distribute the fruit, and enjoy a snack with the children as they play near the water. Be sure to provide appropriate supervision.

NEW TESTAMENT SCRIPTURE INDEX

NEW TESTAMENT THEME INDEX

A

anger—We should be careful what we do and say (Matthew 5:21-22). (p. 15)
anger—Think before you speak or act out of anger (James 1:19-20). (p. 173)

B

Bible—God's Word keeps us healthy and happy (Matthew 4:2-4). (p. 14)

NEW TESTAMENT TEACHING-STYLE INDEX

LEARNING GAMES

Matthew 10:32-33 (p. 19)
Matthew 25:1-13 (p. 29)
Mark 4:35-41 (p. 42)
Mark 10:17-31 (p. 48)
Luke 4:1-13 (p. 60)
Luke 5:1-11 (p. 61)
Luke 14:7-11 (p. 69)
John 8:31-38 (p. 84)
Acts 5:1-11 (p. 99)
Acts 14:8-18 (p. 103)
1 Corinthians 9:24-27 (p. 119)
Ephesians 6:10-18 (p. 137)
2 Timothy 3:1-5 (p. 158)
Hebrews 12:1-3 (p. 171)
1 Peter 1:6-9 (p. 178)
2 Peter 3:17-18 (p. 184)

MUSIC IDEAS

Matthew 11:28-30 (p. 20)
Matthew 18:10-14 (p. 25)
Mark 5:21-24, 35-43 (p. 43)
Mark 15:33-39 (p. 53)
Luke 1:76-80 (p. 57)
John 12:12-16 (p. 86)
John 14:26 (p. 89)
Acts 16:16-34 (p. 105)
1 Corinthians 10:23-29 (p. 120)
Ephesians 4:29-32 (p. 134)
2 Timothy 1:6-12 (p. 157)
3 John 11 (p. 191)
Jude 17-21 (p. 192)

OBJECT LESSONS

Matthew 3:1-6 (p. 12)
Matthew 5:21-22 (p. 15)
Matthew 20:1-16 (p. 26)
Matthew 26:36-41 (p. 31)
Mark 1:1-8 (p. 37)
Mark 4:21-23 (p. 41)
Mark 6:34-44 (p. 44)
Mark 10:13-16 (p. 47)
Luke 2:8-18 (p. 59)
John 1:1-9 (p. 78)
John 4:3-30 (p. 81)
Romans 3:10, 23-24 (p. 107)
Romans 12:1-2 (p. 113)
2 Corinthians 4:13-18 (p. 125)
Galatians 3:26-29 (p. 130)
Colossians 1:11 (p. 142)
2 Thessalonians 3:2-3 (p. 151)
Hebrews 4:13 (p. 168)
James 1:19-20 (p. 173)
James 4:7-8 (p. 175)

PARTIES

Matthew 12:33-37 (p. 21)
Matthew 21:6-11 (p. 28)
Luke 2:1-7 (p. 58)
Luke 14:12-14 (p. 70)
John 10:1-15 (p. 85)
John 15:1-10 (p. 89)
Romans 13:1-7 (p. 114)
Galatians 5:22-23 (p. 131)
Philippians 4:4-9 (p. 140)
Revelation 7:9-12 (p. 194)

PRAYERS AND QUIET REFLECTIONS

Matthew 4:2-4 (p. 14)
Matthew 7:7-8 (p. 17)
Matthew 26:26-28 (p. 30)
Matthew 28:1-10 (p. 33)
Mark 2:1-12 (p. 39)
Mark 14:66-72 (p. 52)
Luke 1:46-55 (p. 56)
Luke 2:41-49 (p. 59)
Luke 23:39-43 (p. 76)
Luke 24:36-45 (p. 77)
John 9:1-12 (p. 84)
John 11:35 (p. 86)
John 18:15-18, 25-27 (p. 90)
Acts 2:1-21 (p. 95)
Acts 12:1-18 (p. 102)
Romans 5:6-8 (p. 108)
Romans 10:10-13 (p. 112)
Romans 15:1-8 (p. 115)
2 Corinthians 2:5-11 (p. 124)
2 Corinthians 6:3-10 (p. 126)
1 Timothy 2:1-3 (p. 154)
Hebrews 1:1-12 (p. 164)
Hebrews 11:1-12, 17-30 (p. 170)
1 Peter 5:7 (p. 182)
1 John 1:8-9 (p. 185)
2 John 5-6 (p. 189)
Revelation 8:3-4 (p. 195)

SERVICE PROJECTS AND MISSIONS

Matthew 5:14-16 (p. 14)
Matthew 16:15-18 (p. 24)
Mark 12:28-34 (p. 49)
Luke 10:25-37 (p. 63)
Luke 16:19-31 (p. 72)
John 13:2-17 (p. 87)
Acts 3:1-10 (p. 96)
Romans 6:23 (p. 109)

SKITS

TRIPS 'N' TRAVELS

Evaluation of *The Children's Worker's Encyclopedia of Bible-Teaching Ideas: New Testament*

Please help Group Publishing, Inc., continue providing innovative and usable resources for ministry by taking a moment to fill out and send us this evaluation. Thanks!

● ● ●

1. As a whole, this book has been (circle one):

Not much help   Very helpful
1   2   3   4   5   6   7   8   9   10

2. The things I liked best about this book were:

3. This book could be improved by:

4. One thing I'll do differently because of this book is:

5. Optional Information:

Name _____

Street Address _____

City _____ State _____ Zip_____

Phone Number _____ Date _____